POEMS,

CHIEFLY ON

THEMES OF SCOTTISH INTEREST.

BY

JOHN TAYLOR.

WITH INTRODUCTORY PREFACE BY

W. LINDSAY ALEXANDER, D.D.

'My heart gaes back to Auld Scotland.'

EDINBURGH: ANDREW STEVENSON.

1875.

INTRODUCTORY PREFACE.

———◆———

I HAVE been requested to write a few lines by way of introduction to this volume. With this request I willingly comply, as I thereby have the opportunity of commending to the notice of the public a work which they will find, I think, worthy of their notice.

The author tells his own story in the Autobiographical Sketch which he has prefixed to his poems. It will be seen from this that he is one of those who have had to cultivate literature under the disadvantages arising from imperfect early education, and amid the difficulties and discouragements of a labourer's lot, and a life of vicissitude and toil. The obstacles which have impeded his course have been of no ordinary kind; but amidst shifting scenes, rude and often rough companions, and constant hard labour, he has manfully striven to cultivate his mind, and has not unsuccessfully courted the Muse. His taste for reading, his sympathy with nature, his love of poetry, and his early Christian training have preserved him from the deteriorating influences to which he has been exposed, and have given a refinement and elevation to his modes of thought and feeling which one hardly expects to find in one who, since he was ten years of age, has had to toil for his daily bread, and who for the most part of his life has had to work as a 'navvy.' His poetical tendency seems to have been born with him; at least it developed itself at so early an age, that he might almost say with Pope,

'As yet a child,
I lisped in numbers, for the numbers came.'

And if he has not needed, like Pope, to invoke the Muse 'to help him through this long disease, his life,' he has in seasons of sorrow and trouble found her his friend and comforter, and has borrowed her aid to brighten seasons of enjoyment or delineate scenes of beauty and sublimity. Without claiming for him any high place among the sons of song, I commend his volume to all who can appreciate and relish genuine, unaffected feeling, true sympathy with nature and man, and pure sentiment expressed in language at once simple and refined.

W. LINDSAY ALEXANDER.

CONTENTS.

———◆———

SACRED PIECES.

AUTOBIOGRAPHICAL SKETCH.

IT has been suggested to me, that along with the following short, unpretending poems, a brief outline of my personal history might not be without some little interest to the 'indulgent reader.' Not that the story of my life presents much that will be thought remarkable or uncommon; but if it should furnish a specimen of the average lot of not a few of our day-labourers,—as I believe it will,—it may lead some who judge harshly of the poor 'navvy' to modify their censure of him, when they come to learn, perhaps for the first time, the amount of hardship he is often called to endure. Rough in speech, as in manner and aspect, he is often as roughly dealt with. A homeless wanderer from place to place, unknown and but little cared for, he must seek employment wherever he can best find it. From his fellow-man he must, as the poet puts it, 'beg leave to toil;' and the 'gaffer,' armed with his 'little brief authority,' is not always the most civil or accommodating of mortals. On the whole, however, and so far as my experience goes, I have found even the class of gaffers not unkindly in their way, but willing enough to do a fellow a good turn when in their power.

I have gone over a great part of Scotland, south and north, through Highlands and Lowlands, and come in contact, more or less, with men of, I may say, all classes in the country, although mixing chiefly with those of my own order. And while I have rarely met with downright unkindness at the hands of any, I can testify that among my fellow-labourers of the pick and shovel I have been for the most part treated as a brother; and seldom have I witnessed anywhere a readier disposition to sympathize with and succour a mate in distress than amongst those sons of toil. Moreover, when Christian and kindly influences are brought to bear upon him, the navvy, ungainly as he may seem, may be so far improved in character as to be no more the outcast he too often is, but a respected, exemplary member both of society and of the Church of Christ. The much-beloved and never-to-be-forgotten Miss Marsh, who has done more for the poor day-labourer than any philanthropist perhaps now living, has amply and most satisfactorily shown what may thus be made of our class through the omnipotence of Christian love, and how through its means the most uncouth and unpromising amongst us may be so transformed as to become meek and gentle as a lamb.

My forefathers, so far as I have been able to trace

them, have been either small farmers, crofters, or humble mechanics. They resided for the most part in that district of Ross-shire commonly known as the Black-Isle, so called from its peninsular form, and the dark-brown heath with which the higher portions of it are covered.

My great-grandfather, William Taylor, held a farm of two pairs of horses and acted as a forester, for a number of years, at Flowerburn, near Rosemarkie. He had five sons. One, named Alexander, spent the better part of his life in the army, going through several sore campaigns on the Continent in the time of the first Napoleon; he was employed in his latter days as a shepherd. Another son, my paternal grandfather, Hugh Taylor, laboured for seven years as a navvy at the making of the Caledonian Canal, where he got married, and after the year 1822 settled in his native parish, where he built a house and held on rent a few acres of land, serving at the same time as ploughman to the Laird of Raddery.

My grandfather on my mother's side, John Munro, was also a crofter and forester for nineteen years on the estate of Raddery. My grandmother, his wife, named Mary Mackenzie, was a native of the parish of Resolis, where her father for many years held a small farm at Agnes Hill.

My father, Donald Taylor, was bred a shoemaker, and at one time employed three men at his business. He also built a house, and had land and a few sheep and cattle; but having caught typhus fever, he died of it, a young man, when I, his only child, was but twenty months old. My sister was born three months after his decease. Thus my mother was left a poor young widow, with two helpless infants, when her married life was little more than begun. I have no recollection of my father, except that I remember wearing, when very young, a pair of boots which I was told had been made me by him. I was then taken to my paternal grandfather's, in the neighbourhood, and was brought up by him and my grandmother; while my mother (though still retaining my father's house and land) resided for the most part with her own parents, also at no great distance. In this way my sister and I were early separated from one another; but as we grew up, we met as often as we had opportunity, and played among the broom and currant bushes in the garden made by our father, which was then falling sadly into decay.

My grandparents were poor, hardworking people, but withal well conducted and pious, who took great pains in instructing me as far as they were able, both in the knowledge and love of God, which they endeavoured to do by example as well as precept. But I was more especially reared under the care of my grandmother, who, while the other members of the family were away, either in service or at outdoor work, would patiently, affectionately, and prayerfully instruct me in the Bible and Shorter Catechism; and at night she would put me to bed, wrap me snug and warm, and kindly teach me short prayers, psalms, and hymns. She was intensely anxious for my eternal good, as she also was for that of the members of her own family. She would pray for us by night and day, and often for each one personally at our bedside while we were asleep. I have seen her repeatedly, after spending a time in secret prayer, return, ere she crossed the door of her chamber, to pray again with increased earnestness. When once told by a Christian friend that such anxiety as hers would injure her mind and bodily health, she answered with emphasis, ' I am afraid they will be lost!' Through the ' Ten Years' Conflict' she was deeply affected by the agitation in the Church, and prayed that divine guidance might be given to her and the Church at large. It was then a most blessed and glorious time in Ross-shire. Dr. M'Donald of Ferintosh, Mr. Stewart of Cromarty, the Sages, Kennedys, and Cooks were all princes in Israel, and the people gathered in tens of thousands from far and near to hear with joy the word preached by these ' Fathers' with wonderful power. At the Disruption, my grandparents and all their family cast in their lot with the Free Church; and I recollect well of going with them to the preaching, which was then held under the open sky, at an old dyke-side, before the new churches were built.

The first years of their residence at Raddery was a time of sore affliction in my grandfather's family, especially to my grandmother, who bore the burden almost alone in connection with a young rising family, five of whom died early, some of them on her knee, with no one near to render any assistance. Through these years my father, her first-born, was a great help and comfort to his mother. But his death gave the crowning stroke to her sorrow; and afterwards, when alone, she would sit at a window, looking toward his house, and utter her overwhelming grief in such words as King David's when lamenting over his son Absalom. She died in August 1849, when I was only ten years old; but I remember distinctly of what was my 'first grief,' to see her wearing away, day by day, to the 'land o' the leal.' And when I would ask her if she was getting better, she would reply, 'If you will be a good boy, I will be better.' I was present when the room was full of friends, gathered at her bedside to witness her last moments; and although her only sister and other friends, newly come from a distance, were present, I was the only one she took particular notice of. I was her 'poor orphan boy,' the son of her darling first-born, and she reached out her hand to me. After I drew near and kissed her, I stood back, with sobs and tears, saying, 'Her lips are cold!' It was the first time I ever felt or saw any one in death. I can never forget the closing scene, as she lifted up her hands and eyes to heaven, as if done with earth, and whispered, in feeble but audible accents, 'Sweet Jesus!'

As soon as I could walk to Rosemarkie, a distance of three miles, I was sent to school there, where I had the advantage of being under superior teachers. I had no taste for what I considered to be dry lessons, such as arithmetic or grammar, but was fond of geography and natural history, or anything interesting in the way either of narrative or poetry; and being naturally light-hearted, I always welcomed my play-hours, when I could, for a short time at least, leave my tasks and enjoy a while with my comrades sporting at the seaside, running over the daisies and gravestones in the kirkyard, or, on our way home in the evening, gathering rasps, 'catching trouts' with our hands, or having an occasional game at 'French and English.'

As I grew up, and was able to do a little work, I used to herd my grandfather's cattle and sheep, and what else I could do about the house and in the fields, generally in the morning before going to school, and in harvest-time during the vacation; and I still remember with what intense delight I was wont, in those days, to gaze on the lovely scenery of hill and dale, field and forest, then spread out before and around me. Across and beyond the corn-fields and 'broomy knowes,' in the immediate foreground of the spot which gave me birth, might be seen the Craigland Hill, covered with a forest of Scotch fir; while in the remoter distance, along the horizon to the north and north-west, stood in silent grandeur the huge Ben Wyvis, and the less huge but stern Ben Vaichard, with many a secluded valley and peaceful glen stretched out between. Far away to the south-east, and across the Moray Firth, might be seen towering up against the sky, and almost mingling with the clouds above, the snow-capped Bel-Rhinnes; while eastward, at no great distance, stood dark and frowning the heath- and pine-clad Kallachie Hill, the gathering mists on which were a sure indication of approaching storm. Impressed and affected with the beauties of such natural scenery, and moved by the traditional memories and stirring songs and ballads of my native country, I would wander about the woods and fields, indulging in all kinds of day-dreams, and attempting even then to express my crude thoughts in rhyme.

It was during my herd-boy days, as I remember, that, having succeeded in stringing together a good many stanzas on some particular subject, to the number of fourteen or thereby, I wrote them carefully out, with the intention, probably, of astonishing grandfather with them as soon as I got home. But taking a fancy to climb a tree hard by, I laid my copy of verses at its foot, to avoid crushing or otherwise injuring the paper in my ascent. I no sooner, however, got up into the tree, than one of the cattle I was herding, attracted to the spot ('Crummie' had a *penchant* for such things), licked up my ill-fated poem, and at one gulp launched it into her remorseless maw ere I could possibly descend to the rescue !

I no sooner mastered the difficulties of reading than I became fond of books. My uncles and other friends used then to lend me such small works as they possessed ; and while attending a Sabbath school, which was held for many years in the house of my granduncle, Andrew Taylor, who with his family and my mother were zealous members of the Independent body, I got there the monthly magazine of the London Missionary Society, the perusal of which afforded me the greatest pleasure; and I shall never forget the interest with which I used to read the accounts it contained of the missionary John Williams, and his graphic descriptions of the South Sea Islands and their savage inhabitants. Some time before 1849, the year of my grandmother's death, I first left home, and lived with my uncle Andrew, who was manager at Avoch Mains, a few miles off. While there, I attended a school for a short time, and spent some of the happiest days of my life; for, besides being amongst pleasant playmates, I was surrounded on every side by rich, lovely scenery, consisting of corn-fields, gardens, thick fragrant woods and hedges, and deep romantic groves, where the lilac and honeysuckle, and numberless rich-scented flowers and blossoms, diffused their perfume on the fresh summer air; while the thrush and clear-ringing blackbird poured their mellow notes through the glades, and the streamlet rippled and sang with unending cadence through the rugged ravine below. To one of my playmates there I afterward expressed my feelings on our childhood in the following piece of irregular composition, which is one of my earlier efforts, and was written to the air of an old sea-song :—

To E. F.

Oh, Elsie, surely you must remember
    Those peaceful days and delightful hours,
When through the wild shady woods we rambled,
    To gather brambles and pretty flowers!

The years of youth they were sweet and pleasant,
    Our hearts were light and our hopes were high;
And oh! we thought they would last for ever,
    When time was gliding so softly by.

But the dear moments of youth are over,
  All, all are fled, like a rosy dream ;
And we may hang up our harps, in sorrow,
  Among the willows by Time's dark stream.

And we may mourn for our hopes departed,
  And for our friends who are passed away,
Whose words could cheer us, whose smiles could
      bless us,
  In youth's gay, playful, enchanting day.

It leaves the spirit so dark and lonely,
  It makes the bosom so sad and sore,
To think that childhood, with all its gladness,
  Is gone, alas ! to return no more.

But, Elsie, why should we sigh in anguish,
  Thinking on visions which could not last ?
Oh, let us pray for celestial pleasures,
  Which bloom immortal when time is past !

BALCONY CASTLE, KILTEARN, 1859.

I afterwards removed with my uncle to Culliss, Nigg,
fifteen miles distant, where I continued to attend school
and enjoy the new scenery. The Chapelhill United
Presbyterian School stands on a beautiful brae-side,
surrounded by bushy banks, green, sunny hollows, and
purling brooks. Our teacher, himself a true poet, and a
kind, genial man, used to give us prizes to encourage us in
making poetry ; and would at times lead a little band of
us up over the hill, through the heather and wild berries,
and down to the shore among the high, frowning cliffs and

wild and solitary dales and caves. I remained at Culliss about two years, enjoying the best of health; and had great fun, especially in harvest-time, when the children and others belonging to the servants on the farm were allowed to glean through the fields. It was delightful for us boys to wander in little bands, gathering the ears of wheat, and on warm days, when tired of gleaning, to go a-fishing, in a deep, broad stream called 'the Canal,' which swarmed with flounders and other sea fishes for miles from the salt water; after which we might be seen returning home, in true Robinson Crusoe style, loaded with corn and fish.

In 1851 I came back to my grandfather's, and in the spring of that year I was employed in the Raddery garden and nursery, scaring birds, where, at the urgent request of an old schoolmate, I composed the first verses of which I have kept a copy in manuscript. From scaring birds I passed (or was promoted, shall I say?) to the grade of stable-boy to 'the Laird,' a post which I held for two years. I may mention that here my superior in office, the coachman, was a sincerely pious man, who daily read and prayed with me, and gave me such good advice as was suited to my age, while I read the history of the *Scots Worthies*, by which I was much impressed; and this, together with the influence of the godly coachman, led me to pray earnestly by myself that God would befriend me, and lead me in the right way.

Here I continued to do a little in verse-making, and began to keep a scrap-book for poems. I had plenty of spare time, and being in a quiet, rural spot, among the bonny woods and gardens and flowery dens of my native place, I 'warbled my native woodnotes wild,' and sang of Wallace and of the heathery hills of Scotland!

I afterwards removed to Cromarty, where I was engaged with a Christian merchant as one of his general assistants, and remained very happy there for more than two years, when health failed me through over confinement.

It was then a heart-stirring time in Cromarty. The minister, the Rev. Mr. M'Eachran, was an active, earnest man, a striking preacher, and unusually fervid in his appeals to the hearts and consciences of his hearers. Not a few, particularly of the youth of the place, were permanently impressed through him, and have ever since been leading a consistent Christian life. Nor will I deny that I myself received impressions of the truth at the time, which I hope will continue to influence me as long as I live.

While at Cromarty I was well acquainted with Hugh Miller's mother, and his 'sister Jeannie,' the subject of one of his poems, and with whose husband, Captain Thomson, a distant relation of mine perished at sea in November 1855. I used to ramble at leisure times among the sea-washed rocks and caverns, and dark, ivy-spread dens, where the gifted geologist and poet spent his early years. And nothing has ever so filled my mind with grand delight as standing among the wild chasms and beetling precipices of that lonely, tempest-beaten coast, watching the tremendous waves dashing in foam and fury, and roaring with a deafening thunder-sound, all along the rugged shore. During my stay in the shop, although damped by the hurry and confinement of business, I composed a few pieces, one of which, bearing on my seaside adventures, will be found inserted among the first of the poems in this volume. Here also, as in the case of the coachman at Raddery House, I was fortunate enough to have a godly companion by day and night, who acted to me as a father. But in 1856 I had to leave, with a constitution to some extent impaired by over confinement; and then, though at home with my paternal grandfather and aunt, where I could breathe the fresh air, and be surrounded by many old friends and the scenes I loved in my younger days, I continued to be more or less of an invalid for two years, in spite of every means that could be used for my recovery. I was then much in company with a young man named James M'Andrew, who also wrote poems. His people and mine were always uncommonly friendly with one another, and many long and delightful excursions he and I have had together, amongst the retired spots about Raddery, and the craggy shores and farmhouses of Belmungie, Lernie, and Berryhill, until he went to Canada, where he got married, and settled down as a teacher. On his leaving Scotland, he presented me with two small volumes of his productions in MSS., as a keepsake. I give the following, from an epistle of twenty-two verses long, which I addressed to him in these our rhyming days :—

Oh ! how time is swiftly flying ;
   Soon this year will have a close ;
Many hearts are lowly lying
   Which in summer stout arose.

Dreary winter hours are coming,
   Bitter days are on the wing,
Lovely flowers to death to summon,
   Once so gay and fair in spring.

And though hope now fills our bosoms,
   Though our hearts are strong and brave,
We are but like summer blossoms,
   Blooming for an autumn grave.

But, my friend, let us remember,
   What no sophist can refute,
Though the flower fades in December,
   Still the life is in the root.

And by His almighty power,
   Who with verdure clothes the plain,
Back returns the tender flower
   When sweet summer comes again.

So in this frail mortal nature
   Burns a flame of deathless fire,
Destined by the great Creator,
   Never, never to expire.

And since He has shone upon us
   With His glorious living light,
And by working faith within us,
   Led our souls to trust aright ;

Through this wilderness of sadness,
　　This wild world of sin and woe,
With contentment, peace, and gladness,
　　Smiling, we can onward go.

And when cold the ' King of Terrors,'
　　Clothed in robes of dread and gloom,
Shall descend upon our spirits
　　With the darkness of the tomb,

We can sink with resignation
　　Calmly on Immanuel's breast,
Trusting in His full salvation
　　For a sweet eternal rest,

With the just of every nation,
　　With the pure of every clime,
From the morning of creation
　　To the funeral-day of time.

At last, by the advice of an old military doctor (the late Dr. Ross, Tain), I spent a few weeks during two warm seasons at the mineral wells of Strathpeffer, where my health and spirits got wonderfully restored. And afterwards, while feeling myself tolerably recovered in health, and gradually increasing in strength, I began doing such jobs of country-work as turned up in my native district, such as gardening and harvest-work; and while engaged among the merry reapers at Raddery Mains, I wrote the piece ' On Scotland,' and several love acrostics to a girl named Mary—a name, by the bye, that seems to be a favourite with the poets. The

New Year's Hymn for 1860, written then while at home, was the first I ever got put into print.

During those years there followed one sore bereavement after another in our little family circle. My uncle Andrew, famed for his horsemanship through a good part of the country, met his death suddenly while experimenting with a strange horse. His father did not long survive him. My only other remaining uncle, David, a shoemaker, and his family were newly gone to America; and my only sister was at the same time laid prostrate with rheumatic fever, which threatened to terminate fatally. However, I was mercifully spared this last stroke, or rather it was suspended till some years after.

In the spring of 1862 I set out for the Falls of Truim, in Badenoch, seventy miles away. I travelled thither partly on foot and partly by the old mail-coach, then running daily between Inverness and Perth. I passed through Strathnairn and other straths on my way, at the season of the year when all was bare and uninviting to the eye, except when the monotony of the far-stretching heath and gloomy woods was occasionally relieved by patches of green meadow and cultivated land. On approaching Strathspey I first caught sight of the Grampians, with Cairngorm white and wintry in the distance. Arriving at Carbridge, as I remember, I had some difficulty in finding lodgings for the night with my bundle on my back; and feeling by this time footsore and weary, I needed rest and harbour. But after being directed from house to house till darkness came on, I was told

at the hut of one poor labouring man, where I called
in hopes of obtaining quarters, that 'there were a great
many vagabonds abroad just then, but they thought
they might keep me.' The vagabonds they meant, I
have no doubt, were the navvies coming and going to the
Highland Railway, which was then in progress between
Inverness and Perth. So I was allowed the shelter of
their roof; and the good woman of the house gave me
brose and eggs for supper, and ditto for breakfast, for
which, and my bed, she charged me but a very moderate
sum, as she handed me back the half of a shilling I
offered her. After accomplishing another good day's
journey, I reached my destination at the 'Falls of
Truim,' eight miles above Kingussie, where I served the
late Misses Macpherson, as gardener, till the year after.
Many of my readers will remember that the house at
the 'Falls' caught fire in 1866, and the last two of the
good old ladies were burned to death in the flames.

The scene of the 'Falls' is surrounded and sheltered
by steep lofty hills, partly covered with birch and
mountain-ash, where the river Truim runs and rumbles
through a succession of abrupt rocky gorges, and tumbles
and foams till it joins the Spey, a mile or two to the
north-east. There grow in abundance the lily of the
valley and many fine and beautiful ferns. There the
wild goats wander and pluck the many sweet flowers
and herbs, the salmon leaps and swims in the dark
pools below, and the hoary eagle flaps his broad
wings far overhead.

On leaving the 'Falls of Truim,' in May 1863, I started on the Highland Railway between Glentruim and Dalwhinnie, where I got employment as a common labourer. I lodged with an old woman in a little turf house, and had for my bedfellow a waggon-driver, who was also my fellow-lodger there; while in the same humble shieling there were two other lodgers besides, consisting of an old English navvy and his wife. The shieling, being near the highway, was frequently visited by tramps and other wayfarers as they passed along. One night a belated wanderer came to the window after all within had been asleep in bed. He tapped at the door and window, and begged for admittance; but the landlady would not open the door at so unseasonable an hour, and told him to be gone. He went away, but after a little returned, insisting on being let in for the night. The dame, however, was firm, and again ordered him about his business. He accordingly passed on, giving no further trouble. But next morning he came in at the now open door, saying he lay all night at a neighbouring farmyard, and asking the woman to boil him some eggs, which he carried in his pockets. This she at once did, giving him at the same time some bread and a cup of tea, after which he lighted his pipe and proceeded on his way. He was not long gone, however, before she discovered that the rogue had passed the night not at the farmyard, as he said, but in an outhouse attached to her bothy, into which he had forced an entrance, and that the eggs she had boiled for him he had theftuously abstracted from her own hencoop!

Here, for lack of other accommodation, we had on an average no less than five miles to come and go every morning and evening to our work, — only this inconvenience was got over so far by our being carried out and back in the contractor's carts. No doubt some temporary huts were thrown up near the works for the use of the men, constructed of the roughest materials, and in most cases after the most primitive fashion; and in these the greater number of them were put up, and allowed to accommodate themselves as they best could. And wonderful it was to see how, by one means and another, they contrived to make themselves comfortable—each feeling, I suppose, in his own way, like Goldsmith's hermit, that

> ' Man needs but little here below,
>   Nor needs that little long ! '

But some rough scenes were to be witnessed among them at times, particularly on *pay-nights*, as may be supposed; or, indeed, on any night when drink was to be had. Then fighting and blasphemy became the order of the day. And not unfrequently it was the same even on Sabbaths; indeed, it was no uncommon thing for the people returning from the churches at Laggan on that sacred day to witness sights of the most revolting description when passing near the huts, and miles away on the road behind the hills. For although no licensed dealer in spirits, so far as I know, supplied the men with drink on Sabbaths, yet they contrived somehow to have it; and it was well known that some women in the neighbourhood of Laggan sold them liquor on the sly as often as it was wanted. And such was the demoralized state of the district during the progress of the works there, that I heard a venerable minister of the place declare from the pulpit, that for the fifty preceding years he had not seen anything so bad. Nor, indeed, is it at all probable that the worthy man should witness the like again in fifty more years, should he live so long. One young man from Aberdeen, a labourer, but not accustomed, it would seem, to such barbarism as prevailed among one of those batches at the time, was so shocked at what he saw and heard, that after working with them for a short time he bundled up and left them.

The truth is, that among our labouring classes, who love 'liberty,' as they call it, and who fancy a life completely free from the restraints of civilised society, find the 'line' to be quite the sphere that suits them; and so they not unfrequently prefer its rough way of living to all other. And rarely is there much done to humanize them when there, or bring them in any way to a better mind. The poor navvy, of all our sons of toil, has perhaps least done for him by the benevolent and Christian agencies of the day, and so has most cause for the complaint, 'No man careth for my soul.' His migratory, unsettled habits and modes of life, however, preclude in a measure all ordinary efforts of that description in his behalf.

I may be allowed to mention that there was at least one Christian lady—Mrs. Colonel Macpherson of Belleville—who took a warm interest in the navvies on the

Highland Railway. I had the honour of this gentle-woman's acquaintance; she condescended to notice me. She invited me to her house, spoke kindly to me, and showed me a fine oil painting of her predecessor on the estate, the celebrated James Macpherson, translator of Ossian. And while talking to me about the navvies and their spiritual condition, so neglected by all, I have seen the good lady hide her face in her handkerchief to conceal her tears, and exclaim with deep emotion, 'Oh! is there nothing can be done for these men?' She gave me as many books as I could read; and years after I had left Badenoch, and while toiling among strangers far away from Belleville, she sent me by post several very valuable presents of books.

I have met with all sorts of characters among my fellow-labourers, from the extreme of boorish or even brutish rudeness, to an amount of civility and politeness such as I have sometimes failed to observe even among 'finished gentlemen.' But the latter, it must be con-fessed, have been few in number as compared with the others. I have at times also remarked, that even the most reckless among them, if gone properly about, are easily prevailed on to give up their wrong-doing, at least for a time. An instance of this kind I well remember, when, coming unexpectedly one Sabbath evening upon a party of rough fellows playing at leap-frog and other boyish games, I went calmly up to one of them, and then to another, and after a few words spoken to each, they gave up their play, and retired quietly to their huts.

Another thing I remember was, that however the nominal Protestants among the navvies were neglected by ministers and others of their own persuasion, the Roman Catholic portion of them were rarely if ever lost sight of by the priest; but, regularly as pay-day came round, 'his *riverence*' was sure to make his appearance, and claim his 'dues,' and in return dispense among the loving children of 'Mother Church' what 'ghostly' service might be needed at his hands.

After I had thus been employed for some time on the works along the Truim side, I was obliged to leave for home, to attend the funeral of a near relative (my maternal grandfather) at Cromarty. And as another branch of the line was being carried on at the time along the northern shore of the Cromarty Firth, I did not go back to where I had been in Badenoch, but asked and obtained employment at these other works nearer home. Here a great number of men were engaged in digging and excavating, with immense labour, a *gullet*, through which the line was to pass. The gaffer I soon found to be a rough, unreasonable fellow, who 'swaggered and swore like a heathen,' so that the poor men who wrought under him had here but a sorry life of it. Besides, the wages were lower and the work heavier than where I had left. They wrought, too, in a reckless, break-neck fashion, with indifferent implements and appliances for the work, and with but small regard for life or limb. One young lad, while working almost at my side, was killed on the spot by a side-fall of clay coming down a bank, and dashing his head with such force against a waggon-wheel as to cause the poor fellow's instant death.

Finding little inducement to remain long here, I was shortly on my way south, back to the Highland line; and I was set to work this time in Strathspey, at filling waggons and driving ballast along the line. Here I was no doubt hard enough wrought, but, to make amends for it, I was pretty comfortably lodged with pious people, who conducted family worship with their lodgers; and on Sabbaths I heard excellent preaching in the Baptist Chapel at Grantown, for although a member of the Free Church, I (along with a cousin of my father, who also laboured on the line) attended the venerable minister, and esteemed and justly celebrated Highland bard, the Rev. Peter Grant, and his son, the Rev. William Grant, who is now pastor of the Bristo Place Congregation, Edinburgh.

But here the line was not long in being completed; so, after I had been in the place but a few weeks, a number of the men were paid off, and I among them, and, much to my regret, I was under the necessity of leaving a locality where I had much real enjoyment, and met with no little kindness from Christian friends. I had then to proceed further up the country to Badenoch again, where on the same line there was still a vast deal of work to be done. Here I got employment, from the summer of 1863, at plate-laying and slope-dressing, until after the railway was opened for traffic, in September of the same year, and afterwards, during the winter, finishing off the line with ballast, etc. Our task was then filling waggons with stones, gravel, and other suitable material, and driving it, with the help of an engine, for many miles along the rails to the various hollows that had to be filled up. This was attended with considerable risk and danger for the workers, owing to the insufficiency, in many cases, of the new-laid rails, which were not as yet properly settled down or duly levelled; nor were the 'box-waggons' very suitable for such use. Consequently a train of such waggons might be seen, heavily laden, with three or four men atop of each, flying along the line, and dancing up and down in the most perilous fashion imaginable, with the engine propelling them from behind, which made the danger all the greater. And one day in particular, I myself made the narrowest possible escape with my life, when thus employed upon a train of waggons that was driven off the rails. The engine-driver and the gaffer had been drinking pretty hard that day, nor ceased till they had emptied some bottles of brandy betwixt them. They went dashing recklessly along with the waggons as described, and the engine-driver being unfit for his work, the gaffer, who was nothing better, tried to manage the engine, when at last the whole of the waggons, with men and material, were pushed clean off the metals. Down went the whole, helter-skelter, in one pitiable heap of wreck and ruin! The men, after being tossed about and torn among the wheels and broken waggons, were carried to their lodgings on '*bogies*' and carts. Many were sorely crushed and bruised; some were sent to the Inverness Infirmary, and some died soon after. At another time the waggons I wrought at were dashed off the rails through sheer carelessness on the part of the engine-driver; they were thrown some yards away from the line, and smashed to pieces. Nor can I to this day recall without horror the ghastly spectacle I then beheld of the men, some of them young, healthy fellows, crushed and mangled in much the same way as I have mentioned before. This occurred near Kingussie, and I remember the inhabitants turned out and gathered around us like a market. Another danger for us, after the line was opened for traffic, was that occasioned by the trains passing us while at work. In this way my gaffer at the plate-laying, having fallen across the rails, had his head as completely severed from his body as if it had been decapitated with the headsman's axe!

At Kingussie, the Spey not unfrequently broke out over the railway banks, not only inundating the works, but carrying great portions of them away. Then the men were turned out by night and day to repair the damage, often under the pelting rain, and wet to the skin. And after many hours at such work, it was rare that we had comfortable lodgings to retire to for food or rest. For my own part, the accommodation I had in the village was of the very worst description—no fire to warm or dry you, be you ever so wet and cold. Indeed, I have seen me go for weeks here with never a dry coat on my back; and as for my lodgings, the place where my bed stood was not only confined, but in wet weather the rain came dripping freely through the roof on bed and floor, so as scarce to allow me space to dress in. So much exposure to wet and cold, and so little comfort within doors, was very disagreeable, and not very favourable for my constitution, which was not robust at the best, and so I was forced to look out for other quarters. I accordingly changed my lodgings, and found it a change considerably for the better, inasmuch as the house was warmer and more commodious. But, alas! in other respects my condition was in nowise improved, but the contrary. Instead of agreeable fellow-lodgers, I had here for my neighbours two fellows who got regularly drunk every pay-night; and though peaceable enough when sober, they no sooner got into their cups than they flew at each other like cat and dog. They would get into grips, and tumble on the floor; then pummel and pound one another till they were weary, and so fall asleep in each other's arms. Then, after a few hours' sleep, they would wake up and be at it again, perhaps at three or four o'clock of a Sabbath morning, at which hour I have been roused somewhat roughly from my slumbers by the two rolling over me in bed, while struggling together in their maudlin, pithless scuffle! I was then obliged after a time to leave this house also, and go to one of the railway huts or barracks, with the carters and waggoners. In the back-side of the hut were six beds in a row, occupied by twelve men, or two in a bed.

The only conveniences I had here were being near my work, and having fine roaring fires of nights, by which I could sit and dry myself when wet, and read when inclined.

The carters are generally found to be somewhat clannish in their own way, not caring to have any in the same hut with them but such as are of like occupation with themselves. Their spare time was usually employed in telling stories of the feats of strength or dexterity performed by themselves or others of their acquaintance, the qualities, good or bad, of the horses they wrought with, or of the masters they had served. Some of them were dog-fanciers, and kept dogs for fighting or poaching, or both; and these they kept chained beneath their beds, to be let loose only when occasion required. Of these, too, the qualities, exploits, and pedigrees formed a favourite subject of discourse. These men I found, however, to be more peaceable on the whole than the navvies generally are in huts, and less addicted to drink. They were exceedingly kind and accommodating to strangers passing the way.

Most of the navvies I have met or wrought with might be divided into four classes—namely, Irish, Lowland-Scotch, English, and West-coast or Skye men. The first I have found to be warm-hearted and generous, but keen-tempered and reckless, especially when they had money to spend. Did space permit, I could furnish some pleasing instances of their generosity towards myself personally when among them. The second are also generous, and will readily help a poor fellow in need if it is in their power. They are more careful of their character and of their money than the Irish, are less excitable, and consequently will bear a greater amount of provocation. The English are frank, and communicative, and off-hand; have nothing to conceal about themselves or others; will rarely pick a quarrel for the mere sake of a row, and will never hesitate to share their last shilling with a mate who happens to be 'hard up.' As for the West-coast or Skye men, they are even more clannish than the Irish, consequently keep more together; and whatever they may be among themselves or their acquaintances, are generally known to be stiff and reserved to strangers. They have small liking for the 'Sassenach,' but less for their brother Celts, the Irish, with whom they have frequent rows, often clearing them off the line when the latter chance to be in the minority. But, on the other hand, when Pat gets 'more power to his elbow,' and gains the ascendancy, he is not slow to retaliate on his cousin the West-coast man.

After the opening of the line, in September 1863, most of the contractors' horses having been taken to Edinburgh and sold, many of the carters at Kingussie left also; and while one young lad and I were the only occupants of the hut, I wrote and got published some rude verses, of which the following selection may be taken as a specimen :—

The railway is finished, the engine is on,
Away from the Highlands the navvies are gone,
Right south to 'Auld Reekie,' to see something new,
So we to Kingussie must all bid adieu !

Our hut, so delightful on dull rainy days,
Where the drivers have sung by the splendid red blaze,
Will no more be a shelter, when lodgings are scant,
For the traveller, hungry, and drowsy, and faint.

The navvies are hardy, and reckless, and bold,
But Badenoch is weary, and dreary, and cold,
And the bare lofty mountains are mantled in snow,
O'er the wastes of Drumochtor, where hurricanes blow.

In the lands of the stranger, wherever we rove,
There is comfort and happiness, friendship and love ;
But few feel or care for the navvies so bold,
Unless they have pursefuls of silver and gold.

When first to the railway I wandered away
From my home and my garden and roses so gay,
My aunty advised me, and told me 'beware,'
For the rough ones would teach me to gamble and swear.

But my thoughts and my notions she could not control,
For hardship and danger was life to my soul ;
And nothing could conquer the bent of my mind,
For to search and discover I still was inclined.

So I left my own valley, where soft waters shine ;
I joined the wild navvies to work on the line,
And dwell far away in the stranger's rude home,
Where the bleak mountains rise and the brown rivers
    foam.

It is pleasant, while years with their changes roll on,
To live in a corner and call it our own,
With hearts true and gentle our fortune to share,
To soothe our affliction and banish our care.

The ploughman who bears the cold blast and the shower,
The gardener who tends the green herb and the flower,
May run all their wearisome griefs to beguile,
By friendship's kind hand and affection's bright smile.

The fisherman far o'er the fierce flying foam,
On the high-swelling billow may think of sweet home,
And in peace and contentment with rapture can rest,
When he gladly returns to his dearest one's breast.

But navvies are severed from all silken ties
Which link and lift mankind to love and the skies,
And surrounded by ills on the pitiless wave,
Which hurry men downward to death and the grave.

We are far, far away from the hills and the braes,
And the faces we loved in our earlier days ;
And, alas ! we are frail, when the current is strong,
To steer through the treacherous waters alone.

No sister to watch us in sickness is near,
No father to counsel, no mother to cheer,
Or guard us, or warn us to keep from the path
That leads to temptation, destruction, and death.

Yet cheer, brother workmen ! though proud ones may
      frown,
Our cause and our colours shall never come down ;
Although we are strangers, regarded by few,
We help one another, as Christians should do.

Oh ! let us be earnest, and steady, and strong,
Looking patiently upward while moving along.
His arm is almighty, and clear is His eye,
Who sustains, guards, and watches the low and the high.

A navvy is constant, whatever may blow,
His heart ever kindles with charity's glow ;
He sticks by his mates when their pockets are bare,
.And of his last shilling he gives them a share.

Our feelings are bright as the moon's gentle form,
And strong are our hearts like the oak in the storm ;
Compassion and loyalty beat in our breast,
And surely poor navvies are men like the rest.

Then steam up your waggons, 'drive on, lads, I ho !'
We fear not the tempest, we heed not the snow ;
The pick and the shovel shall conquer the sword,
Independence and honesty reap their reward.

Conducted by heroes like dauntless Mackay,
And trusty M'Donald, with strength in his eye ;
And Gowans, a champion stedfast and true,
Like the ' Iron Duke ' in action at hot Waterloo.

We can level the mountain and tunnel the rock,
And scatter their fragments like ashes and smoke,
Till civilisation and commerce shall run
And bless every nation beneath the bright sun.

I remained at Kingussie, as I have said, until the
finishing of the line ; after which I came into Inverness,
and there obtained employment during the remaining
winter months, until, in March 1864, I returned to Kingussie to attend a garden and nursery, but was forced to
leave there in November of the same year in ill health,
after suffering much during the summer and autumn
through weakness, occasioned by living in a damp,
unhealthy house. The scenery of Badenoch around

Kingussie is savage and grand, with terrible rocky mountains, deep wild glens, strong rapid rivers and cataracts,— scenery which is the very soul of poetry. There I composed the 'Ode to the River Gynack,' to which I invite the attention of my Highland friends and others; besides 'The Berry-bush,' 'Why shrink, Old England?' and the piece 'To Jessie,' my dear friend, who now lies in her grave in the beautiful larch and mountain-ash sheltered cemetery at Kingussie.

After leaving Kingussie, I crossed the Grampians for the first time, visited Blair-Athole, Killiecrankie, Dunkeld, Perth, and Scone; and, to fulfil an old promise, I went to the village of Pitcairngreen, five miles from Perth, near the Almond Water, to see the friends of a man who lost his life on the Highland Railway by being run over by a goods train, and I wrote for his sorrowing widow a long elegy on his death. After visiting, along with some friends, the graves of 'Bessy Bell and Mary Gray,' some cairns, and other interesting and romantic spots near the Almond, I returned north, partly to visit the few relations I had there, but chiefly to see my only sister, who was now in very delicate health. At that time, while at home with my aunt 'Nanny' at Raddery for the last time, I could well enter into the feelings that dictated the lines of the poet, when he says that,

> 'To one fatigued wi' close employment,
>   A blink o' rest's a sweet enjoyment.'

I could not, however, afford to remain long in idleness; and so, after going to see cousins and other friends of my father's at Tarbat, and in Sutherland, I must bethink me of retracing my steps southward again, in order, if I could, to obtain employment at the railway then being constructed betwixt Methven and Crieff. My mother accompanied me on my journey the length of Fort George Ferry, where, as I remember, I saw a poor man with his three motherless children, the youngest scarce able to walk, thus far on his way with them from the far North to Glasgow, to which he was proceeding on foot. His finances had failed him, so that he had not wherewith to pay his fare across the ferry; and he was hanging about the pier till some one should take pity upon him, and supply him with the necessary pence. My own funds, too, were sufficiently low at the time; but the poor fellow's case seemed so pitiable that I could not resist my inclination to help him, and so I shared with him the little I had, to ferry him over. I then wrought my way south as I best could, doing any little jobs that cast up, so as thus to earn what should carry me to my destination. Among other places on the road, I stayed for a short time at Dumphail, near Forres, where I was employed wheeling heavy stones and wet gravel across the Findhorn,—work not very unlike that referred to by Burns' 'Luath' as the occasional occupation of the labouring poor, who, he says, are

'Whiles fashed eneuch,—
A cotter howkin' in a sheugh,
Wi' *dirty stanes* biggin' a dyke,
Barin' a quarry, an' sic like.'

C

Nor was the handling of 'dirty stanes' the worst of it; the work was heavy as well, and not unattended with danger, for the stuff had to be wheeled across the river upon narrow and by no means very steady planks. And not unfrequently the stream, in time of rain, came tumbling down deep and strong; at which times it was 'gey kittle' work to steady oneself and the heavy-loaded barrow on the yielding plank, when, with the least loss of balance on either side, one would be sure to tip over, barrow and all, into the flood below. Indeed, one of the men, an old soldier, who was worn out with long service, and was but ill fitted for such hazardous work, did actually one day fall over, and narrowly escaped being carried down the river and drowned. The other men, for some reason best known to themselves, did not take to the poor man; and if they had no direct hand in bringing about the mishap, they at least did not seem to regret it.

My next job was at Forres, in a bone-crushing mill, where I remained for a few weeks. I was partly induced to do so on account of my sister being then an inmate of the hydropathic establishment there, to which she was ordered for her health, and where, though my means were but slender, I had to maintain her to the best of my ability. It was here, too, where I bade her farewell for the last time, and where I saw her last in life. At the bone-mill I was employed only as a supernumerary hand; and so, my engagement being temporary, I was soon on the tramp again. I therefore started, not for the Crieff Railway, as I had formerly intended, but for the Aberdeen Waterworks, which were then being constructed, and to which I resolved meanwhile to proceed in preference to the other.

On my way to Aberdeen, while travelling through a number of towns and villages and many interesting spots, by way of Keith, Buckie, Banff, Huntly, Inverurie, etc., I formed some few poetical acquaintances. One young man, a shoemaker, named William Donaldson, since then published a volume, entitled *The Queen Martyr, and other Poems*, and very kindly sent me a copy as a present. In the romantic village of Marnoch I also enjoyed the privilege of hearing the gospel preached, and saw the Lord's Supper dispensed by the late Rev. Mr. Hendry, Free Church minister there. After leaving Turriff, I saw Benachie. A few verses I wrote on that famous hill will be found inserted in another part of this volume.

On arriving at Aberdeen, I proceeded up Deeside to Banchory-Ternan, where part of the waterworks were then being carried on, and I at once obtained such employment as was to be had there at the time. One of the tasks assigned to me, along with some other men, was blasting and tunnelling through a stiff, hard rock, at which we wrought almost without intermission for six months together. And such was its extreme hardness, that often a good shot of powder, well 'stemmed,' would not remove a capful of the rock; and not unfrequently I have seen a deep bore, the weary work of many hours, primed in the usual way with the strongest blasting powder, and the shot when discharged passing out of the hole as clean as if from the mouth of a cannon, with not so much as an ounce of the stubborn material displaced. This was an operation at once wearisome and dangerous; and one poor man, while at the same work in another tunnel a little farther up on the waterworks, had the misfortune of getting both his eyes blown out, as well as sustaining at the same time several bodily injuries besides. A sum of fifty pounds was raised for him on the works, and he now travels the country with a barrel-organ, presented to him by some friends in Inverness, and with which I see him sometimes in the streets of Edinburgh, led by a daughter.

While at Banchory, I have often had my 'solitude sweetened,' especially on Sabbath mornings, at the Deeside, where, far from all the solace of home, I could quietly read my Bible and Spurgeon's *Sermons*. Here I also had the advantage of attending the Rev. Robert Reid's Sabbath class, as also his public services in the Free Church there. These I enjoyed much, and likewise the special services got up in the place by the late excellent Colonel Ramsay of Banchory Lodge on behalf of the navvies, and frequently conducted by himself, as well as by clergymen and others whom he got to address them. The death of this Christian gentleman and 'devout soldier,' which took place while I was in the district, was universally lamented, and by none more than by the navvies, to whom he was a true friend. My own feelings on the melancholy occasion I endeavoured to express, though very inadequately, in the few lines I have dedicated to his memory, and which will be found in the present volume. While at Banchory I also wrote the pieces entitled, 'The Sigh of the Stranger,' 'On the Approach of Summer,' and a long rhyme on the lodgings I fell into there. As it is no fiction, but a chapter of my own personal experience, and a picture of such places as the poor navvy must make up his mind to meet in with at times, I venture to present the reader with part of it :—

THE MODEL LODGINGS AND LANDLADIES
OF HAMMERMAN SQUARE.

A TRUE STORY IN RHYME FOR NAVVIES.

COME, all ye bold navvies, who travel and toil
Through England and Scotland and Erin's green isle,
I'll spin a long *yarn*, if ye sit ye down there,
About the wild women of Hammerman Square.

I am a *green tramp* from the county of Ross,
Where my grandfather dwelt by a Highland peat-moss;
But little I thought, when a ' young fellow ' there,
Of the terrible women of Hammerman Square.

I have lodged in *wee towns* through the north and the
    south,
Between the ' Fair City ' and Cromarty mouth;
But in Perth or in Paisley there's none to compare
With the thundering fierce women of Hammerman
    Square.

For cooking or washing they are little worth—
Their trade is frivolity, gossip, and mirth ;
They talk and they tattle, and none can declare
All the games and the *daidos* of Hammerman Square.

And then for the beds and the lodgings they keep,—
You may go to repose, but you get little sleep ;
For the rats and the *varmint* that dance but and ben
Would make you as nervous as granny's grey hen.

At church or at chapel they never appear—
Their god is their belly, their pleasure is beer ;
And blind silly *flats* are soon *snapped* in a snare,
If they mind not the dodges of Hammerman Square.

They kick up a row, and they swear, drink, and fight,
And like tigers they roar till the morning grows bright ;
'Tis a rare habitation, deny it who dare—
'Tis a hell upon earth in the Hammerman Square.

When I came to Banchory weary one day,
On Friday a fortnight before the last pay,
The day when the navvies got ten *bob* of *sub*,
I only had sixpence to get me some grub.

As down by the waterworks I took a walk,
With Forbes the gaffer I had a long talk ;
I thought by his beard he was surely a Turk,
But he spoke very civil to me about work.

After 'knocking about' through a part of the day,
I inquired about lodgings at one Mrs. Rae ;
She said, 'You're a tramp,' and she guessed I was bare,
And show'd me a lodge in the Hammerman Square.

I asked if the lodging was decent and clean ;
She told me she knew not, she never had seen,

But strangers and *tramps* on the top of the road
In Hammerman Square should take up their abode.

Thinks I, my old lady, 'tis all in mine eye ;
A *navvy* requires to be *trampish* and fly,
That he of all *straw-yards* and quacks may beware,
And no' be *sucked in* in the Hammerman Square.

With that to the Hammerman Square I did creep,
And round the old corner I shortly did peep,
To try for the lodgings she sent me to there,
A rough raffle den in the Hammerman Square.

I stood and looked in at the horrible door,
I saw and I listened, but wanted no more ;
If this be the fashion, I need little care
To take up my lodgings in Hammerman Square.

I was *hard up* for *tommy*, I wished for a rest,
So back round the corner I turned to the west ;
Next door to the tailor's I lodgings found there,
But, alas ! I was still in the Hammerman Square.

My money all spent, I was worthless and queer,
With nothing to help me and no one to cheer ;
And *tick* was denied me in storehouse and shop,
For I was a stranger, and then I might *slope*.

For a while I had nothing to eat but dry chuck,
Which gave me poor courage to drive out the muck ;
But soon I got money to keep me in grub,
From the King of the navvies, the great Mr. Gibb.

With patience I wore all my hardships away ;
And when I got pennies my lodgings to pay,
My kit in three minutes I bundled with care,
And left the *old* jiggers of Hammerman Square.

And now I am lodging back up in the 'Neuk,'
With one Mrs. Taylor, as snug as a duke;
Where I get peace and freedom, and plenty fresh air,
And am glad to be clear of the Hammerman Square.

Bad luck and the toothache to old Mrs. Rae,
Perhaps I may thank her on some other day;
For my soul or my body she little did care,
When she told me to lodge in the Hammerman Square.

Ye warm-hearted mothers, who may have a son
Rambling about through the country alone,
Remember, advise them that they may beware
Of the 'tow-rows' and 'forges' of Hammerman Square.

Now all brother navvies, who, passing this way,
May look out for lodgings on some future day,
I tell you take warning, I bid ye beware,—
Oh! risk not your life in the Hammerman Square.

Wherever you wander, be sober and true,
And follow improvement whatever ye do;
Let virtue and love in your bosoms abide;
Let peace be your comfort, and wisdom your guide.

Although we are navvies, I bid you reflect,
If upright we walk we will still gain respect;
We can cherish pure feelings, and stand for the right,
And show by our conduct that honour is bright.

I continued to be employed in connection with the
waterworks at Banchory till they were fully completed,
which was in the earlier part of 1866. I went thence to
Aberdeen, in quest of whatever work might cast up, and
soon succeeded in obtaining employment, it being the

spring season, when day-labourers are most in demand about towns. The house I lodged in I found to be that in which Lord Byron lived with his mother, when a boy attending the Aberdeen Grammar School, viz. No. 64 Broad Street,—a part of the 'Granite City' then deemed fashionable, though now it is sadly fallen from its former repute.

I had not been many weeks in Aberdeen when I was found out by some of the men who had been my fellow-workers at Banchory; so nothing would serve but I must throw up my work and accompany them to West Calder, near Edinburgh, where a branch of the Caledonian Railway was then in progress. Accordingly we all took steamer to Granton, and proceeded thence to our proposed destination, where we were at once set to work on the line. It was coarse, hard labour we were put to; and that was to be expected, for when is it ever otherwise with the poor navvy? He, more than most men, has to earn his bread by 'the sweat of his brow;' nor does he utter any complaint on that score! But then the labourer is worthy of his hire; and if by unfair means he is cheated out of it, or of any portion of it, the wrong-doer is not only chargeable with injustice, but with cruelty as well, inasmuch as robbing a poor man, whose sole property is the labour of his hands, is more heartless and heinous than doing the like wrong to a rich man, to whom the loss is probably but a trifle. Such was our feeling at West Calder, when on pay-days our receipts were several shillings less than we had wrought for, and that not on one or two occasions, but many times in succession. This was attributed to mistakes on the part of the time-keeper; but the contractor would not hear our complaints, and would give us neither satisfaction nor redress; consequently after a time I left the railway, and took employment in Young's Paraffin Oil Works, in the same locality.

Here I laboured for more than two years, partly with the joiners and saw-millers, and partly underground with the miners; and once I had the misfortune of sustaining a very serious and well-nigh fatal bodily injury. While at work at one of the shale-pits, a heavy bolt, or piece of metal, falling accidentally from above, near the pit's mouth, struck me with great force a little behind the crown of the head, causing a severe contusion, and all but fracturing the bone. Of course I was stunned by the blow, and rendered for the time insensible. I was conveyed to the Edinburgh Royal Infirmary, where I lay in great pain and weakness for several weeks, during which time I lost a large quantity of blood. But skilful treatment on the part of the doctors, and kind attention from the nurses and others, with the blessing of God, restored me gradually to a measure of health. So, when sufficiently recovered to resume work, I returned to West Calder. While I lay in the Infirmary, hundreds of men had been paid off at Young's works, through a dulness in the paraffin oil trade; consequently work was scarce. However, I was then taken to labour in a quarry connected with the railway; but I found it too much for my strength, which was quite exhausted ere I had wrought above two hours. I accordingly told the 'gaffer' that I felt myself unfit as yet for a day's work, and must therefore give it up. Being, however, a kind, feeling man (with whom I was previously employed in the same quarry), he advised me to continue at it, working, if not for a whole day, then for a half day, more or less, just as I was able; and assured me that I would sooner regain my lost strength by doing a little work daily than by remaining entirely idle. Nor was the worthy 'gaffer' mistaken, for after two half-days' work I felt able for that of a whole day, and continued so during my stay in that place.

West Calder is naturally a very healthy locality, although the air is now much poisoned by the smoke and gases which proceed from the pits and oil works abounding in all directions through that part of the country. The chief retreats of my leisure hours while there were in the 'auld kirkyard,' or out of the village among the little woods and burns, and, when time permitted, the Pentland Hills. My chief productions at that time were the 'Lines to an only Sister after receiving her Picture from Home,' 'Feed my Sheep,' and 'Bonny Mary o' the Glen.'

In the spring of 1868 I removed to Edinburgh, where, during the first two years, I lodged in the Grassmarket, sleeping in a small apartment with a full view of the Greyfriars' Kirkyard, which I enjoyed exceedingly, especially on clear nights, when the trees, monuments, and crumbling tombs were all beautifully mellowed under a flood of moonlight, and the low night-wind crept and rustled over the impressive silent scene,—a scene sanctified and immortalized by the sufferings and the dust of hundreds of Scotland's most noble martyrs. Here I have wrought in a nursery for some time, and latterly obtained employment at the levelling of the Meadows, where I have now laboured with the spade, shovel, and barrow for the last six years. And it is worthy of note, that several of my fellow-workers are closely connected with famous events in Scottish history. One is great-grandson to that Semple who bore the standard of the Covenanters at Bothwell Brig. Another, named Rankin, is descended from one of the few who escaped with their lives from the massacre of Glencoe. And still another of them is a respected elder in one of our United Presbyterian churches in town, and is the third in direct descent in his own family who has held the same honourable office—his grandfather, John Common, whose name he bears, being an elder in one of our earliest Dissenting churches in the south ; besides a second cousin of the poet Burns, an Ayrshire man, named James Niven. His mother, Jane Rainy, was Burns' full cousin, and often shore together with her gifted relative on the same 'hairst rig.' While a fifth had been precentor in the first Free church, that at Marnoch. He led the singing there during the first eight years, his services beginning on the first Sabbath it was opened. All of these my fellow-labourers are intelligent, decent men, and though humble their lot, and obscure their daily task, yet I can enjoy their company, and try to gather wisdom at their feet, especially when, as is not unfrequently the case,

> ' They lay aside their private cares,
> To mind the kirk and state affairs ;
> They'll talk of patronage and priests,
> Wi' kindling fury in their breasts.'

My only sister died at Inverness on October 12, 1871. On the evening of that day, while at my usual work in the Meadows, there was telegraphed to me the sad news, and next morning I took train for the North, and there found my mother watching by the bier of our beloved. She lies buried in the beautiful cemetery of Tomnahurich. I had not been at home for seven long years before; so, ere returning to Edinburgh, I visited the scenes and acquaintances of my boyhood, in the Black Isle and Easter Ross; and there I found many to welcome me, but changes were visible on every hand. Many familiar friendly faces were gone; hearths at which I was once a welcome guest were now cold and cheerless; and the home of my childhood was in ruins. With the exception of my aunt 'Nanny,' who now resides in Fortrose, and who is ever ready to give me a hearty reception, all my near relations now living are scattered by sea and land, in America and elsewhere; and here am I in Edinburgh with my aged mother. While I think of my friends and countrymen, the Highlanders in general, I am forcibly reminded of the words of Byron's Hebrew maid :

'But we must wander witheringly,
In other lands to die;
And where our fathers' ashes be,
Our own may never lie.'

In drawing thus my short and simple narrative to a close, I may mention that, with the exception of the few 'Sacred Pieces' at the end, the poems in this volume are arranged in the order of date, the last pieces, beginning at 'Highland Music,' being my Edinburgh pieces, which comprise about as many as all the others which I publish put together. During my earlier years I wrote few pieces, and even of them I only publish a small number. The reader will observe, that since I began to dip into verse-making, I have been for most part away from home; but owing to the constant enjoyment I have had with the Muse, I have always managed to preserve copies of my effusions; and, gentle reader, 'such as I have give I thee.'

POEMS.

POEMS.

TO A ROCK ON CROMARTY SHORE.

GREAT monument of power divine,
   Deep planted in the sea !
Oh ! if I had a choice of spot,
   My home would be on thee.

When billows rage with wrath sublime
   Around thy rugged base,
There how enraptured would I sit,
   And on the tempest gaze !

Or when the bark before the wind
   Is drifting o'er the foam ;
Or when the fisher spreads his sail,
   And steers his course for home.

D

Or when the sea-bird, wild and free,
  Is screaming through the caves,
Or floating finely with her mate
  Among the breaking waves.

The sea-bird sits on thy grey cliffs,
  And mocks the dashing foam;
For high above the ocean's rage,
  The sea-bird has her home.

Oh! if I had a lowly cot,
  Built near the gurgling tide,
How oft would I with fervent joy
  Ascend thy stately side!

To ponder on the heaving waves,
  That swell and dash and roar
Around the splendid cliffs and caves
  Of Croma's rocky shore.

Free from the world, with all its cares,
  Its tumults, and its strife,
With nature's wild romantic scenes,
  How calm would pass my life!

And should I visit distant climes,
  Where fairer scenes are seen,
Where flowers are always fresh and fair,
  And hills are ever green,

I'll ne'er forget 'Macfarquhar's bed,'
    Lashed by the stormy sea,
Nor Cromarty's old hoary rocks,
    Though rough and rude they be.

CROMARTY, *November* 1855.

———o———

TO A YOUNG FRIEND.

DEAR Mary! thou art blithe and young,
    Now are thy precious golden hours;
For time shall blight thy bloom ere long,
    That nips the comely lovely flowers.
Then, Mary, lend an earnest ear to me,
While I relate the simple truth to thee.

When Summer's gentle dew is seen
    On springing grass and daisies fair;
When lambkins gambol on the green,
    And larks with music swell the air;
We little think on dark and stormy days,
When gloom shall overspread our Highland braes.

So, in youth's sweet enchanting day,
    When splendour decks the dazzling bowers;
When health and vigour make us gay,
    And heedless glide away the hours;
We little think those pleasures may be brief—
May soon be dimm'd with sickness, care, and grief.

The stately thistle and the rose,
　That bud and blossom bright and gay,
And every charming flower that grows,
　Shall fade in winter's waning day;
And so shall every earthly beauty die,
When we shall from this crumbling body fly.

But *piety*, that flower divine,
　It thrives in sadness and in joy;
More precious than the diamond-mine,
　Its value time shall ne'er destroy.
Planted and ripened by the Saviour's grace,
Its lustre frosty time can ne'er efface.

And death's devouring woeful gust,
　That withers every mortal bloom,
That lays youth's courage in the dust,
　And strength and beauty in the tomb,—
E'en in its darkest, coldest, fiercest hour,
It cannot mar this pure immortal flower.

But, like the lily on the plain,
　That parts with all its blasted flowers,
To rise and flourish fair again
　With April's bright reviving hours,
It casts aside its wasted coat of clay,
To shine expanding in celestial day.

Then, Mary, pray sincerely now,
  That *He* would plant this flower divine
In thy young heart who can bestow,
  And round thy soul its graces twine;
For every earthly flower is doomed to die,
But this shall bloom through all eternity.

RADDERY, *April* 1858.

———o———

SCOTLAND.

SCOTLAND! my noble fatherland!
  Though I am doomed to toil,
I feel I am a freeborn child
  While I can tread thy soil!

I sigh not for fair Turkish skies,
  Or soft Italian bowers;
I envy not Australian gold,
  Or long for Indian flowers.

Thy peaceful fields, and rocks, and towers,
  Lashed by the endless sea;
Thy hills, and woods, and mountains grand,
  Are all the world to me.

I think of thy great sons, who bled
   And died in olden time;
Who gave to me sweet liberty,
   And made their lives sublime.

I read how Ossian's mighty soul
   Was moved with scenes of old;
Of young Malvina's starry eyes,
   And Fingal strong and bold.

I muse along the flowery vales,
   And press the heathy sod,
Where noble Wallace fought so true,
   And dauntless Douglas trode.

'With all thy faults,' my native land!
   Thou sitt'st amidst the foam,
For the oppressed a resting-place,
   And for the free a home.

The music of thy Sabbath bells
   Revives my fainting breast;
They call me to the better land,
   Where troubled souls shall rest.

RADDERY MAINS, *October* 1861.

———o———

VERSES FOR A FRIEND ON RECEIVING A SISTER'S LIKENESS.

' The memory of joys that are past,
  Pleasant and mournful to the soul.'—OSSIAN.

THRICE welcome, little lifeless form !
   Though silent, thou art dear ;
For the kind one you represent
   Remembers me sincere.
I see a loving sister's face,
   Although now far away,
Who nursed, and watched, and guarded me,
   In childhood's helpless day.

What glowing, stirring memories
   Within my soul arise,
As with an overflowing heart
   I gaze on those sweet eyes !
My thoughts, with more than lightning-speed,
   Fly back to summer hours,
When on the braes of Cromarty
   We ran and gathered flowers;

When through the woods we wandered far,
   And by the lonely shore,
Through the wild rocks and dark old caves,
   To hear the ocean's roar.

Oh! scenes of cloudless happiness,
   When friends and comrades dear
Would soothe our little sorrows, and
   Our tales of mirth would hear!

Oft, oft I sigh, and fondly wish
   For those glad days again,
When our young spirits felt no care,
   Our merry breasts no pain.
But now, alas! our early hopes
   Are overspread with gloom,
And many joys are withered,
   No more on earth to bloom.

Our parents, by the hand of death,
   Were riven from our side,
And through this world of sorrow we
   Are scattered far and wide.
The house which was our home still stands
   Close by the sounding sea,
Where long ago we spent our years
   In love, and peace, and glee.

But He who wisely overrules
   The works and ways of men,
Does all things for His glory; oh!
   Why should we murmur, then?

His precious volume tells us of
　　The people of His love;
From all their tribulations they
　　Shall rest at last above.

In life and joy eternally
　　They shall surround His throne;
Their woes shall be forgotten, and
　　Their fears will all be gone.
Then may we walk with patience in
　　The footsteps of our Lord,
And ever, like our fathers, trust
　　His mercy and His word!

RADDERY.

————0————

ON THE DEATH OF A FAVOURITE DOG.

WHERE the heather sweetly grows,
　　And the wild wind freshly blows,
By the river's sparkling wave,
There behold a lowly grave.

All his wanderings now are done,
His last race of mirth is run;
Cold the heart and dark the eyes,
Which could feel and sympathize.

Feet which, like the nimble roe,
Scaled the mountain's craggy brow,
Now no more can wander free,
Far through woodland, field, or lea.

When the sun's last beam of day
O'er the Benyan fades away,
Much I love alone to roam
Where the thundering waters foam.

But no more, with willing feet,
Tweed will gladly run to meet,
Or again convey me back
Past the Truim's rocky track.

FALLS OF TRUIM, BADENOCH, 1862.

———o———

ON THE SCOTTISH HEATHER.

I DEARLY love the heather bloom,
  I love its fragrant rich perfume;
For oft, in youth's delightful days,
On my beloved native braes,

I've wandered careless, free, and wild,
A healthy, happy, fearless child,

Dreaming away my summer hours
Among a thousand mountain flowers.

Like the wild bee, far far from home
In ecstasy I loved to roam ;
And sweetly dear o'er all the rest,
I loved its opening purple breast.

In winter, by the blazing fire,
Beside my hoary, sage grandsire,
I've listened to romantic tales
Of Caledonia's hills and dales.

And while warm blood my breast does fill,
My freeborn Highland soul shall thrill
To think of bards and heroes bold,
Who nobly sung and fought of old.

On earth, whate'er may be my lot,
My youth will never be forgot,
When through the heather, like the bee,
With loving ones I wandered free.

FALLS OF TRUIM, BADENOCH, 1862.

AN ACROSTIC.

M y dearest Mary now is far away,
A cross the fathomless, wild, trackless sea ;
R eturning spring will make all nature gay,
Y et without Mary what is all to me ?

D own through the den I now may muse alone,
A nd, where the faded flowers are wrapt in snow,
V isit the grove where, round the mossy stone,
I ncessantly the clear soft waters flow.

D reary and lonely are my days and hours,
S ince my beloved is beyond the main.
O h, Mary ! have you left those peaceful bowers,
N o more to bless me with your smile again ?

RADDERY MAINS, *October* 1861.

———*o*———

OUR FADED FLOWER.

' A rose's brief bright life of joy,
  Such unto him was given.'—HEMANS.

A WAY, away, in his flowery prime,
      When sweetly the moments glide,
From his mother's hand and his father's knee,
And his brother's and sister's side.

Away, away, when his path is strewn
  With beauty, and mirth, and love,
We trust from the cares and snares of earth,
  To our Saviour's home above.

Where the fair, the great, and the good repose,
  They have buried his lovely clay;
Where the hoary vast cathedral stands,
  While centuries roll away.

The sigh of the tender may arise,
  The tear of the brave may fall,
For him who shall run with his mates no more,
  Nor answer his cousin's call.

Though science shone on his noble soul,
  And genius inspired his breast,
His brow is not for the bard's green wreath,
  Nor his crown for the soldier's crest.

He died like the snowdrop pure, that fades
  When the birds begin to sing,
In the angel's garden of life to bloom,
  'Neath the smile of an endless spring.

KINGUSSIE, 1863.

TO THE MATE OF MY YOUTH.

' Dear are the days of youth ; age dwells on their remembrance
  through the mist of years.'—OSSIAN.

BELOVED young mate of my childhood, you know
    All things we confide in shall perish below ;
The young and the beautiful wither away,
And the dearest we love must be laid in the clay.

In the days of our childhood, when little we knew
But to gaze o'er the valleys and mountains so blue,
And sing like the wild birds with boundless delight,
Through the fields, and the green woods, and primroses
        bright ;

Oh then, when our bosoms were cloudless and free
As the fair summer sky and the calm summer sea,
In deep meditation we often would long
For distant lands famous in story and song.

We knew not the world, with its trials and snares,
Its toils and its troubles, its sorrows and cares ;
For the dear ones we loved were so constant and kind,
That our young hearts were light as the fresh mountain
        wind.

There was peace in our dwellings and beauty around,
While far through the rocks like the goats we would bound ;
By the steep crags of Eathie, and Lairnie's rough shore,
To linger and muse where the ocean waves roar.

If we trode o'er the uplands or sailed on the sea,
To the tempest's loud music we listened with glee ;
And the dark-waving pines, and the proud-rushing streams,
Awakened our raptures and kindled our dreams.

With our dogs through the heather and beautiful ferns
We have herded our cattle among the grey cairns,
Where flowers in profusion adorn the sweet scene,
And grandeur, and silence, and solitude reign.

But our youth, with its sunshine, and pleasure, and play,
Like April's bright blossoms, is vanished away ;
And our comrades, who joined in our rovings of yore,
Are scattered o'er many a far distant shore.

Like the flowers of the garden when July is green,
The beauty of man in life's summer is seen ;
Like the flowers of the garden in winter's cold gloom,
All mankind departing return to the tomb.

Although we still languish for comfort and peace,
And our sighs and our longings shall never decrease,
This world can afford us no lasting relief,
No ease for our trouble, no balm for our grief.

Then let us to Jesus for pardon repair,
For hope and true gladness are found only there;
Oh! let us for grace and for mercy now run,
For this weary sad journey will shortly be done!

Our souls He can bless, and our sins wash away;
Let us pray for His Spirit, and make no delay,
For many redemption impatiently spurn,
And leave the green pastures no more to return.

How dreadful, how woeful, how mournful to stand
At last on the Saviour's mighty left hand,
And be driven away from His glory in heaven,
To anguish, and gloom, and despair unforgiven!

Our fathers who smiled on our childhood are gone,
And through the world's strife we must battle alone;
Yet we need not repine for the loss of their love,
But think of our home and our Father above.

That father has tenderly kept us till now,
As no other friend could protect us below;
And no one can picture what He has in store,
But His own shall be with Him when time is no more.

Then why should we wander in dark pathless ways,
When Israel's great Shepherd so lovingly says:
'Ye spirits, who pant for what earth cannot give,
Come, drink of the heavenly fountain, and live'?

KINGUSSIE, 1863.

THE LITTLE MAIDEN.

A MERRY, blue-eyed maiden,
　In all youth's loveliness,
Grows up beside her father's hearth,
　Her mother's life to bless.

Sweet innocence and beauty
　Shine on her forehead fair,
Which tells of a fond mother's love,
　A watchful father's care.

But time shall work sad changes,
　Earth's gladness will not last ;
And mute the silver harp may be
　Ere many years be past.

Then may the grace of heaven
　Her youthful soul adorn ;
For glory may her age be ripe,
　Like a full ear of corn !

Almighty, Holy Spirit,
　Renew her tender heart ;
And save, oh, save her from the snares
　Of hell's deceitful art !

E

Too soon, alas ! the tempter
   Begins to lure us down,
To share with him eternity
   Under Jehovah's frown.

But Saviour, triumphant,
   Thy people's glorious King,
Who died and rose to quell our foes,
   And leave in death no sting,—

Oh ! may the little maiden
   Be sanctified by Thee ;
Under Thy banner may she rest
   Now and eternally.

52 CASTLE STREET, INVERNESS,
   January 1864.

————*o*————

TO JESSIE.

COME, Jessie, come ; the ev'ning breeze
   Breathes cool and calm among the trees,
Spreading sweet fragrance from the flowers
Among our Highland mossy bowers.

Come, Jessie, come ; the mountain stream
Shines with the sun's declining beam,

And far within the leafy wood
The wild dove coos in solitude.

Now is the hour for love and song,
When music echoes loud and long ;
When little birds pour from their throats
Thankful, heart-thrilling, artless notes.

Oh ! let us shun the busy street,
Where guile, and mirth, and folly meet ;
And let us seek the peaceful glen,
Far from the homes of weary men.

Oh ! there the stately pine-tree rears
Its lofty crest, unbent by years ;
And slender ferns and saplings weep
In grandeur o'er the rocky steep.

There, in the lonely shady dell,
The violet unfolds its bell,
Where the pure summer dew may rest,
Like virtue in a gentle breast.

Oh ! Jessie, come, although the rose
On thy fair cheek no longer glows ;
For sickness, like the withering storm,
Has nipp'd thy tender youthful form.

Kind nature, where her beauties shine,
Will teach thy spirit truth divine,
And whisper softly to thy breast
Delightful dreams and hopes of rest.

KINGUSSIE, *May* 1864.

———*o*———

WHY SHRINK, OLD ENGLAND?

LINES WRITTEN DURING THE WAR WITH DENMARK IN 1864.

WHY shrink, Old England, from the path
 Of glory? why so crouch thee down?
Have nations ceased to own thy wrath,
 And fear the thunder of thy frown?

With lion-hearts to sweep the field,
 And 'Hearts of Oak' to rule the wave,
How could thy awful spirit yield
 To act the coward or the slave?

England! thy ensign, o'er the seas
 So long in triumph safely borne,
Now floats but tamely in the breeze,
 The cruel, haughty despot's scorn.

And will Old England bow the head,
  And will Old England bend the knee,
And draw no more the battle-blade
  That trampled kingdoms may be free?

Must Italy's and Hungary's cry,
  And Poland's groans of deep despair,
And Denmark's solitary sigh,
  Vainly implore thy help and care?

O thou, the hope on every shore
  Of all who pine for liberty!
Arouse thee, as in times of yore,
  That patriots still may cling to thee!

Bethink thee how thy sons of might,
  Thy fearless Nelson, Moore, and Blake,
Could trust in God and do the right,
  Till sullen tyranny would quake.

England, awake! Oh, never let
  The hapless perish in their woe;
For thou, though strong and proud, may yet
  Be friendless, desolate, and low.

KINGUSSIE, *August* 1864.

———o———

'THE POET.'

SUGGESTED BY READING VERSES IN AN ENGLISH PAPER.

WHO welcomes first the op'ning flower,
That blushes on the rural bower,
Refreshed by April's genial shower?
The Poet.

Who loves the little merry bird,
Whose sweet song in the wood is heard
When leaves by summer winds are stirred?
The Poet.

And who rejoices, full and free,
The fields and shining streams to see,
When autumn glows o'er land and sea?
The Poet.

When winter stern in awful form
Wraps hills and glens in clouds and storm,
Who smiles and burns with rapture warm?
The Poet.

When lilies droop and violets die,
And roses pale and withered lie,
Who sings their memory with a sigh?
The Poet.

Who prizes dearly while below
One kindred soul, where he may go
For solace in his deepest woe?
                    The Poet.

Who wishes all divinely blest,
And tries with sympathetic breast
To help the wretched and distrest?
                    The Poet.

Our fallen world is full of woe;
Who grieves to see the noble low,
But hopes the tryant's overthrow?
                    The Poet.

Who softly walks with solemn tread
On spots where sacred dust is laid,
To weep in secret o'er the dead?
                    The Poet.

When Luna lights, in beauty drest,
The silent river's trembling breast,
Who yearns for everlasting rest?
                    The Poet.

KINGUSSIE, *August* 1864.

————0————

THE BERRY BUSH.

' When bards are removed to their place ; when harps are hung in
Selma's hall ; then comes a voice to Ossian, and awakes his soul ! '—
OSSIAN.

THE berry bush grows green within
    The garden fresh and fair,
Where I can go at eventide,
    To breathe the healthy air.

I love, I love the berry bush—
    Its graceful branches run,
With thickening leaves and clustering fruit,
    Before the ripening sun.

For when my daily toil is o'er,
    And I can think and talk,
In the cool shade I often muse,
    Along the gravelled walk.

Here I can spend in joyful rest
    The balmy eventide,
O'er some rich, glowing, friendly page,
    With loved ones by my side.

Here I can gather all my friends
    Since this big world began—
The soothing flowers and guiding stars
    Of weary, wandering man.

Beloved Cowper, sweet and mild,
  Affliction's mournful son !
Who now in cloudless glory bows
  Before Jehovah's throne.

Hugh Miller, truthful and profound,
  Whose words like diamonds shine ;
Delightful Wordsworth, fresh and free ;
  John Bunyan, sound divine.

Dear gentle Hemans, England's rose,
  Fragrant with love and youth,
Telling to childhood's blooming heart
  Warm tales of joy and truth.

Milton, who like an angel dreamed ;
  And Byron, king of song,
With spirits like the thunder-cloud,
  Dark, dread, sublime, and strong !

Bold Ossian, whose wild harp was strung
  In days of kingly strife ;
And great Columbia's bright bard,
  Who wrote the ' Psalm of Life.'

Here I can melt in thrills of joy,
  And laugh in bursts of glee,
With Shakespeare's jewels, bright and rare,
  Spread o'er a boundless sea.

Here I can grieve for hapless Burns,
  And sigh for lovely White,
Till feeling overcomes my heart,
  And tears bedim my sight.

Here I can taste the waters pure,
  And feel the living fire,
Searching the wondrous, glorious page,
  Whose lights can ne'er expire.

The mighty seer who marched between
  The Red Sea's waves of wrath,
And trode Mount Sinai's awful slopes,
  Along the lightning's path.

Daniel, wise and wonderful,
  Beautiful and divine,
Whose echoes of eternity
  Sound through the mists of time.

John, in lone Patmos banished far,
  Where mighty waters foam,
Who saw (in visions grand and fair)
  The saints' eternal home.

The same unbroken strain is sung,
  The same good story told,
By all those poets wild and grand—
  The holy men of old.

O Thou, the Guardian of the pure,
   The Shepherd of the free !
Teach me to love my fatherland,
   Teach me to follow Thee !

Oh ! give me patient fortitude,
   And meek humility,
That I with love may honour Thee
   While I on earth may stay.

Grant me an honest, grateful heart
   For all Thy blessings given,—
Thy precious gifts and liberties,
   And the sweet hope of heaven.

But now along the woodlands green
   Eve's gloomy shadows fall,
And now the chill wind brings the roar
   Of stream and waterfall.

One look around the berry bush,
   One glance across the West,
One farewell, and we all retire,
   In our warm home to rest.

KINGUSSIE, *September* 1864.

———0———

ODE TO THE RIVER GYNACK, NEAR KINGUSSIE,

THE SCENE OF A HIGHLAND CLEARANCE.

'Families by hundreds were driven across the sea,' etc.—KENNEDY.

DARK stream of the valley, swift rolling in pride !
    Oh! stern are the mountains that stand by thy side,
Where the cloud and the mist move along on the blast,
Adorning with grandeur each hoary old crest.

But where are the warriors, fleet as the roe,
Who arose like the torrent to burst on the foe,
When the clansmen for battle were proudly arrayed
With the sword and the plume, and the pipe and the plaid?

Dark stream of the valley, swift rolling in pride !
Oh ! fine is the heather that blooms by thy side,
And lovely in summer the beautiful dew
May shine in the bell of the violet blue.

But where are the warm-hearted, sweet, blushing maids,
Who tripped o'er the moorlands and smiled in the shades,
When virtue and charity, honour and truth,
Grew strong in the loyal bosom of youth?

Dark stream of the valley, swift rolling in pride !
The bird of the wilderness sings by thy side ;

And still may the bard in free solitude stroll,
With the fire and the rapture of song in his soul.

But where are the patriarch fathers, who trode
Glen-Gynack with love to the Bible and God,
Who poured on the breath of the calm Sabbath air
The heart-melting psalm and the heavenly prayer?

Dark stream of the valley, roll on in thy pride,
Thy waves will soon mingle with Spey's rushing tide;
And soon to the ocean thy waters will sweep,
To melt in the foam of the fathomless deep.

And the brave and the kind have been scattered afar
From the glens their bold forefathers guarded in war;
And alas! but the shadow the stranger may trace,
In a spiritless, faithless, degenerate race!

Dark stream of the valley, swift rolling in pride,
The heart-broken patriot sighs by thy side;
Caledonia, ruined, is bleeding and torn,
Though once she was fair as the Queen of the morn!

And rashly the hunter treads over the floor
Where the sons of the mighty were cradled of yore;
Though grass on the paths of our ancestors grows,
He feels not, he weeps not, for Scotia's woes!

Dark stream of the valley, swift rolling in pride!
Oh! pure are the fountains that gush by thy side;

And fresh is the fragrance that floats on the air,
Where the larch and the willow wave handsome and fair.

But alas ! the sweet life-giving verdure is vain,
For wild desolation is spread o'er the plain ;
The rocks and the woodlands and fields of the glen
Are vocal no more with the gladness of men !

Dark stream of the valley ! the cliffs by thy side
Have long to the sound of thy thunder replied,
And changes have passed since thy flowing began,
And changes will pass in the future of man.

And the proud and the lowly, the rich and the poor,
Are all hastening on to eternity's shore ;
But rich is the pasture and lovely the rest,
Where the wrath of the tyrant can never molest.

KINGUSSIE, *October* 1864.

---o---

TO THE HILL OF BENACHIE,
ABERDEENSHIRE.

WELCOME, thou hill of Benachie !
    Oft have I wished to gaze
Upon thine ancient hoary head,
    Wrapped in its misty haze.

It is not that thy cliffs arise
　　To heaven, and stretch away ;
Or that the heather blooms and waves
　　Around thy summit grey.

It is not that from off thy heights
　　A prospect may be seen
Extending far on every side—
　　Fine fields and valleys green—

(The rivers broad and burnies bright
　　Of Banff and Aberdeen ;
All onward to the open sea,
　　With waving woods between).

But by my grandsire's warm fireside,
　　When but a lisping boy,
Old songs of Scotland I have learned
　　To sing with deepest joy.

And one was dear to man and maid,
　　And dear it was to me,—
A sweet, melodious, melting strain,
　　'The Lass o' Benachie.'

Oh, while I bear a Scotchman's name,
　　I'll cherish evermore
Our native songs of honest love,
　　The bosom gems of yore.

In all their sweet simplicity,
  Old Scotland's songs for me !
And dearer still I love the strain,
  ' The Lass o' Benachie.'

———o———

AN ACROSTIC.

I n summer, when roses and violets bloom,
S weet, sweet is the breath of their fragrant perfume,
A nd the tints of their beauty are lovely and fine ;
B ut what is their sweetness and beauty to thine ?
E very stir, every echo and musical sound,   [profound,
L ingering soft through the shades of the woodlands
L ives still in my bosom, my woes to beguile ;
A nd so the remembrance will be of thy smile !

R emembrance will shine, while I rove on the wild,
O n me like a sunbeam, refreshing and mild ;
B right visions will haunt me, delightful and pure,
E ver teaching my spirit to hope and endure.   [shower,
R ound thy rude home, though fast flies the cold mountain
T he primrose blooms fair on the green lonely bower ;
S o may virtue and happiness aye be thy guest,
O utspreading in comeliness over thy breast.
N ow I bid thee farewell ! May you ever be blest !

KILLIECRANKIE, *February* 7, 1865.

VERSES

ACKNOWLEDGING KINDNESS AT A SOIREE GIVEN BY THE
INHABITANTS OF BANCHORY TO THE NAVVIES ON THE
ABERDEEN WATERWORKS, SEPTEMBER 21, 1865.

THE time draws nigh when we no more
    The Banchory hills may see ;
But we will think, when far away,
    Of lovely flowing Dee.

And we will bless for evermore
    The village by the stream,
Where dwell the gentle and the kind,
    Our gratitude who claim.

Weary and friendless and unknown,
    Through many lands we rove,
Divided from the kindred hearts
    And joys we dearly love.

Far from the hills and flowery fields,
    Where first in youth we trode,
We roam a barren wilderness,
    Along a thorny road.

But roses soft and lilies fair
    Along our path are found,
Delighting us with melting smiles,
    And perfume shedding round.

F

Bright eyes of beauty shining sweet,
　And hearts that warmly glow,
Dispelling clouds of human care,
　And soothing human woe.

This evening by the burning light
　With rapture we combine,
To meet with warm, congenial souls,
　Kindled by love divine.

Then let us here with beating breasts
　Our grateful homage tell,
While joyful tones of melody
　And thrilling music swell.

May we remember, when we meet
　To mingle in our mirth,
Our Father of one blood hath made
　All nations of the earth.

'And let us pray that come it may,'
　Like sunshine from above,
The day when man shall care for man
　With universal love.

The navvy in his timber hut,
　The sailor on the sea,
The peasant in his peaceful home,
　The Indian wild and free,

The wealthy and the lowly poor,
   The simple and the wise,
Are one to Him who lives and reigns
   Our Saviour in the skies.

Oh! let us prize the noble truth
   That teacheth us to love,
That makes us like the lion bold,
   And gentle as the dove.

And let us love the precious faith
   That tells of sin forgiven,
And cherish in our hearts the hope
   To meet with God in heaven!

20th September 1865.

———*0*———

LINES

SUGGESTED BY THE DEATH OF THE LATE COLONEL RAMSAY
OF BANCHORY LODGE, WHO DIED THERE, NOVEMBER 6,
1865, LAMENTED.

WHEN warriors fall asleep,
   The brave may weep,
And glowing bards attune the trembling lyre,
To sing of glorious souls of quenchless fire,
   And give the hero's name
   Enduring fame.

And when the Christian dies,
And upward flies
With radiant angels on triumphamt wing,
The sighing Church to God may praises sing,
For ransom'd spirits bless'd
With holy rest.

O Ramsay ! o'er thy tomb
Fair flowers shall bloom,
Sweet with the fragrance of thy deeds of faith ;
Thou hast departed, beautiful in death,
Bright as a setting star
O'er seas afar.

A patriot-soldier thou,
Noble and true,
Oft hast thou grasped Britannia's shining steel ;
Yet, lovingly, thy gentle heart could feel
And pray for those who roam
And seek not home.

In melting sympathy,
From every eye
Soft tears shall fall for dear ones fatherless,
And for thy lady, lonely in distress,
Who mourns a consort good
In widowhood.

Thy bounty and thy care
The poor did share,

The stranger tenderly thou didst regard;
Now incorruptible is thy reward,—
    An heritage above,
    A feast of love.

    The little flock shall meet
    In concord sweet,
To drink of springs whose waters overflow,
And trim their lamps as Zionward they go;
    But thou art no more here,
    The faint to cheer.

    On Canaan's tranquil shore,
    Thy voyage o'er,
Thou hast ascended at the Master's call.
Oh, may thy mantle on a brother fall!
    The victory is won;
    Thy work is done.

BANCHORY, *7th November* 1865.

———*o*———

THE SIGH OF THE STRANGER.

OH! dull is the prospect and dark is the day,
    When summer's bright verdure is wither'd away;
But now is the season when over the soul
Sweet visions of memory lovingly roll.

The tempest is driving along the dark sea
That severs the 'Isle' of my fathers from me ;
But love lights my soul as I gaze o'er the foam,
And I think of the past and the dear ones at home.

Ye hills of my fathers ! I sigh for the west,
Where the heather-bell blooms o'er the warrior's breast,—
The land of the mountain, the mist, and the snow,
Where the river rolls pure through the valley below.

For there is the land of my love and my dreams,
Where in youth I have mused by the gurgling streams,
Where the ash and the holly, the pine and the oak,
Wave in majesty o'er the dark sides of the rock.

Dear land of the Sabbath ! where multitudes meet
With the Bible, to worship in harmony sweet.
Oh ! when shall I listen, as when I was young,
Where the songs of our Zion in Gaelic are sung ?

While hearts full of love in the Highlands remain,
To hail the return of the rover again,
Sweet love lights my soul as I gaze o'er the foam,
And I think of the past and the dear ones at home.

BANCHORY, *January* 1866.

———o———

ON THE APPROACH OF SUMMER.

FAIR summer is comin', sad bosoms tae cheer,
 Fair summer is comin', the pride o' the year,
Whan the gentle wee birdies will sing their sweet tune,
Wi' hearts fu' o' gladness i' the fine month o' June.

Fair summer is comin', sae fresh an' sae braw,
Young floweries will blossom, saft breezes will blaw;
The beans an' the clover, the thyme and the broom,
On the warm breath o' July will pour their perfume.

O Scotland, our country, thy hills we ha'e loved,
Where free an' licht-hearted in youth we ha'e roved,
An' sat i' the sunshine, auld stories tae tell,
Where grow the white gowan an' bonnie blue bell.

In the times o' our fathers, whan ilka fireside
Was free o' dishonour an' misery an' pride,
An' love strong an' simple, an' tender an' true,
Pour'd its balm o' pure gladness like the cool mountain dew.

An' aye thy green meadows, where hums the wild bee,
An' clear-shining burnies that run tae the sea,
Tae thy laddies an' lassies will ever be dear
Till life's latest moments, wherever they steer.

Then awa' let me daunder where the win' whispers free,
An' plays o'er the waters an' the banks o' the Dee ;
An' gaze, while I muse i' the calm, lanely den,
On the dark distant summit o' high Clochnaben.

The trees I ance trusted are withered an' bare,
An' the roses I cherished shall flourish nae mair ;
An' the strains o' my spirit are blent wi' a sigh
For hame i' the regions that never shall die.

But Scotland, tae thee, while the seasons return,
A fire in my breast shall unceasingly burn ;
An' my love for thy martyrs is stronger than death,
For thy soil has been soaked in their blood for their faith.

BANCHORY, *April* 1866.

———0———

TO MY ONLY SISTER.

AFTER RECEIVING HER PICTURE FROM HOME.

> ' Oh ! blest be thine unbroken light,
>   That watched me as a seraph's eye.'
>   BYRON.

SISTER, my muse is wild and plain,
    But thou wilt hear my humble strain ;
Its breathings still are dear to thee,
In all their rude simplicity.

For love has linked thy soul to mine
In trusty bonds of truth divine,
Constraining thee to long for me,
And sigh while I shall absent be.

The wasting years are rolled away,
Like wintry clouds in bleak array,
Since last I gazed, and breathed farewell
To all in Raddery's blooming dell.
The years of youth, with all their glee,
Will come no more again for me ;
And quench'd are many gladsome beams,
That charmed me then with thrilling dreams.

A father's care no more I know,
For those who loved me long ago
Slumber in silence side by side
By old Rosemarkie's beating tide.
Only in fleeting gleams I see
The ancient ' Isle,' so dear to me,
Where I have sung in early days,
While bounding through the broomy braes.

But while in distant climes I stray
From thee, Jemima, far away,
I grieve not for the faded past,
Though o'er my heart a chill is cast ;
I only bow submissively
Before high Heaven's majesty,

And look by faith to life sublime
Beyond the gloomy gates of time.

'Tis there alone we look for rest,
'Tis there our spirits shall be blest;
'Tis there our hopes, which withered lie,
Shall bloom to immortality;
When we shall gain the deathless shore,
When we shall sin and mourn no more,
When we IMMANUEL shall behold,
And tread the streets of polish'd gold.

No more I roam in high delight
The dark *Moal-bhui's* breezy height,
Through green Ardmeanoch's lonesome fields,
To gather fruits the moorland yields;
For now, 'mid southern prospects tame,
Far from the glens I love to name,
Unsolaced by a kindred smile,
An orphan stranger I must toil.

No more I rove through *Raddery Den*,
To ponder far from human ken,
Where flows the cool, unsullied stream,
Deep shelter'd from the scorching beam;
But now I move amidst the crowd,
Whose sound is turbulent and loud,
Where tainted is the Lowland vale,
Where noisome vapours load the gale.

No more I stand where billows roar,
On Ethie's winding rocky shore,
Where gipsies dwell in darksome caves,
Lulled by the thunder-sounding waves.
And dearer still, alas ! no more
I linger by the cabin door,
To view the mountains of the west
Ere evening shades invite to rest.

While steering on the world's wide sea,
Come rushing o'er my memory
Old scenes and legends of the strand
Of my romantic fatherland.
And while the stranger's couch I share,
The stranger's board, the stranger's care,
For the sweet light of home I pine,
Which never on my soul may shine.

The navvy's heart is warm and brave,
Like those who sail the stormy wave;
Though daily dangers round him fly,
Oh, fearless is his daring eye.
But on his heart there is a string
That sweetest music forth can bring,
If touched to tremble skilfully
By the soft hand of sympathy.

Nursed where the rocks of SKYE are seen,
Or midst old IRELAND's valleys green ;

Or by bright ENGLAND's gentle rills,
Or CALEDONIA's misty hills,—
But whisper of a sister's care,
To him for ever pure and fair,
And bursts the hidden spring of love,
Which all his home-born feelings move.

So, sister kind, Jemima dear,
Thy brother sheds the secret tear,
While months and seasons silently
Are passing fast and solemnly.
Not that dark danger's path I tread,
Thereon to earn my daily bread;
Not that misfortune's dreary shade
Has early settled on my head.

'Tis that thy form, so full of light,
Has come to bless my languid sight,
But in dull sickness or distress
Thy warm soft hand I cannot press.
'Tis that thy voice, in accents clear,
No more at morning's dawn I hear;
That thy dear eyes, so sweet for me,
No more at evening's close I see.

While in the image of thy face
Thy lineaments I clearly trace,
Home-sickness calls me oft to mourn,
And I to thee would fain return.

Thine is the breast of sympathy,
That still has warmly felt for me
With love that ne'er shall cease to glow,
Whatever storms may coldly blow.

Oh! while the Lord my life shall spare,
May He still bless me with thy care,
A gentle star my path to bless
Throughout this gloomy wilderness.
And in the hour of death be near,
My spirit with thy words to cheer,
To whisper of the pleasures sweet
Abounding where we hope to meet.

WEST CALDER, 1866.

———o———

VERSES TO MR. DAVID MORRISON,

NIGHT WATCHMAN, CALDERVALE; AUTHOR OF 'THE WEE
THACK HOUSE,' ETC.

SING, noble bard, like the wild woodland warbler!
    Sing of the beauties of green Caldervale!
Though destined to pour, while thy dear ones are dreaming,
    Thy sweet, gentle strains on the chill midnight gale.

Cold is the heart as the snows of December,
 Dull is the bosom like dead senseless clay,
That feels not the charm of thy warm soothing numbers,
 That owns not the power of thy heart-thrilling lay.

Sing, noble bard ! like the pure cooling fountain
 That peacefully rises and gurgles along,
Wherever thy musings may silently wander,
 Let the weary be strengthened and cheered by thy song.

Sing of the joys of the poor and the lowly,
 Of true wedded love and the raptures of home ;
Sing of the land of our stern mighty fathers,
 Where Clyde onward flows to the wild western foam.

Where, by the dark rocks in the echoing valley,
 Bold Ossian tuned 'neath the pale moonlit skies
His soft-sounding harp, while he sang with emotion
 Of heroes and maidens with 'slow-rolling eyes.'

Where the grey lonely cairn on the wild silent moorland
 Reminds us our ancestors conquered of yore,
And slaughter'd the Dane and the proud cruel Roman,
 Who dared to intrude on our pine-covered shore.

Here is the land of the kind manly ploughman,
 And his 'dear Highland Mary,' of deathless renown ;
His laurels of fame shall immortally flourish,
 And bright are the gems of his world-honour'd crown.

The land of the lake and the loud-roaring torrent,
  The gay waving thistle and broad tartan plaid,
Embalm'd in the love of the brave dauntless hero,
  Enshrined in the breast of the free fearless maid.

The land where the Bible and calm holy Sabbaths
  Are the bulwarks of all that is sacred and fair,—
The dear lovely land of our own happy childhood,
  The country that claims our affection and care;

Where the great name of Knox, and the strong daring
    Wallace,
  Are the watchwords of freedom by mountain and dell;
Where the ashes of Cameron and thousands of martyrs
  In sunshine repose 'neath the bright heather bell.

Sing, noble bard! by the cold sullen waters
  Oh! hang not thy harp on the sad weeping tree,
But move every chord till thy spirit awaken,
  And sorrow will vanish like clouds o'er the sea.

Thy soul may be bruised like a flower in its fragrance,
  Bruised by affliction and blighted by scorn,
But thine are no more than the hard fiery trials
  Thy true-hearted fathers have patiently borne.

Sing, noble bard! while the roses are dying,
  And lilies and violets no longer appear;
Sing! while the breezes of autumn are sighing
  (The bard loves the breath of the fast-fading year).

For the hopes of his life like the sere leaves are falling,
   And lonely he pines like the mild yearning dove,
Till a springtime revives with a beauty eternal,
   Where night never falls on the daylight of love.

ADDIEWELL, WEST CALDER, 1866.

———o———

THE WHITE WEE FLOWER.

ANEATH the hawthorn on the knowe,
   There grows a white wee flower,
That mak's me think o' a' things sweet,
   An' beautiful, an' pure.

It has a slender, bendin' stalk,
   An' slender, weepin' bells ;
The emblem o' true innocence,
   O' spotless worth it tells.

If my true love was by my side,
   As she is far awa',
The white wee flowerie I wad pu',
   White as the driven snaw ;

An' ower her bonnie youthfu' brow,
   Sae peacefu' an' sae fair,
The white wee flowerie I wad twine,
   To deck her silken hair.

Green are the braes o' Addiewell,
　　An' bricht the Lowland bowers,
Whare I can muse in solitude
　　Amang the white wee flowers.

But lanely is my friendless heart
　　For ane wha's lo'ed me lang,
Wha's meltin' voice o' melody
　　Could cheer me wi' a sang.

The mountains o' my fatherland
　　I mayna see again,
That proudly rise in grandeur, o'er
　　The stormy northern main.

Fortune an' fame may on me fa',
　　But joy can nae be mine,
Till I can claim the maid that dwells
　　Whare Highland waters shine.

WEST CALDER, 1866.

——*o*——

BONNY MARY O' THE GLEN.

BONNY Mary o' the glen,
　　I like to see her face,—
The beauty o' the Clachan braes,
　　The flower o' a' the place !

G

Her glossy hair is aye in trim,
   Her cheeks are bricht an' clean ;
She's lovely in her modesty,
   An' tidy as a queen !

Bonny Mary o' the glen,
   Whan summer days are lang,
She gangs aside the whirlin' burn,
   An' sings her gentle sang.

She comes for water to the spring,
   She gangs to milk the kye ;
And aye her heart is merry, like
   The birdies i' the sky.

Bonny Mary o' the glen
   Has twa sweet beamin' een,
Sparklin' like the draps o' dew
   That glitter on the green.

Her bosom, wi' the love o' youth,
   Beats warm an' tenderly ;
Oh, may she never tine her joy,
   But blyther may she be !

Bonny Mary o' the glen,
   My lay to thee is sung ;
Oh, may thy life be ever pure,
   Although thy heart is young !

The flower that opens tae the licht
   Aside the summer sea,
Amang the rocks, is comely, fresh,
   An' beautiful, like thee !

WEST CALDER, 1866.

———o———

SUMMER SMILES ONCE MORE.

WILD Winter, wrapped in gloomy robes,
   Has left our northern bowers,
And Flora reassumes her throne,
   To reign the queen of flowers.

Young daisies deck our Scottish braes,
   And fields, and meadows o'er,
With beauty, light, and loveliness,
   While Summer smiles once more.

The 'lily of the valley' spreads
   Its perfume through the dell,
Stirring the spirit of the bard
   Like a celestial spell.

The tender dove, the sweet cuckoo,
   In mellow concord pour

Delightful music through the grove,
  While summer smiles once more.

The ocean and the silent lake,
  The river's moving stream,
Sparkle beneath the soothing light
  Of morning's lovely beam.

Nature her beauties doth display
  Around our native shore;
All things of life are full of joy,
  While summer smiles once more.

WESTWOOD.

———o———

HIGHLAND MUSIC.

A PRIZE POEM IN THE 'PEOPLE'S JOURNAL' FOR CHRISTMAS
1869.

OH, give us music sweet and clear!
  Oh, give us music deep and strong!
The stirring strains we love to hear,
  Blent with the majesty of song.

Oh, give us music grand and high,
  Till every chord reverb'rate o'er

With the wild martial minstrelsy
　Our fearless fathers loved of yore ;

The strains that fired the men of old,
　As on they marched to meet their foes !
Our valiant clansmen, stout and bold—
　The Campbells, Camerons, and Munros.

The tempest drives along the sea,
　And rages through the forest tall,
While in affection's circle we
　Are gathered in the lighted hall.

With lightsome bosom, full of mirth,
　Contented, happy, gay, and warm,
We meet around the blazing hearth,
　And listen to the lashing storm.

When Ossian sang his strains sublime
　In days of glory and renown,
The Gaelic maids of olden time,
　With bosom fair and tresses brown,

Attuned the harp's wild trembling string
　To melting songs of love and war,
And chiefs and bards, in clustering ring,
　Rehearsed their deeds in lands afar.

So, while in friendship we combine,
　Like blythsome birds in yonder grove,

Rebecca's fingers, white and fine,
   Along the chords of music move;

To pour inspiring melodies
   To captivate th' enraptured soul,
Like thrilling sounds of throbbing seas,
   That through dark ocean caverns roll.

Oh, give us music, while the smile
   Of gentle woman softly glows!
To cheer, to comfort, and beguile,
   Like perfume of the budding rose.

Oh, give us music!—tender tones,
   Mild as the murmuring of streams;
Or solemn as the wind that moans,
   Sad as our long-forgotten dreams.

It soothes the soul to joyous rest;
   It bids the warrior's fear depart;
It warms the lover's swelling breast;
   It fills the bard's deep yearning heart.

EDINBURGH, *January* 1868.

ORPHANS.

ALAS! the days we love are fled,
   The dear, delightsome days of yore !
Alas ! our father's halls we tread
   With joyous, bounding hearts no more.

No more, when winds are sounding high,
   When wildly drives the drifting snow,
We meet, with mirth and melody,
   To hear the tales of long ago.

No more we range the breezy shore,
   No more we walk the woodlands through ;
No more we climb the uplands, o'er
   The distant western hills to view.

In balmy days, when tender flowers
   Are sweetly bathed in early dew ;
When morning lights the mountain bowers,
   And gilds the ocean, broad and blue.

Each green, romantic, silent dell,
   Each corrie, calm, and deep, and lone;
Each gloomy, fairy-haunted cell,
   Where sobbing waters rush and moan ;

The cliffs where wave the sombre pine,
  The hazel, beech, and birchen tree,
For ever dear to thee and thine,
  For ever dear to mine and me ;

High rocks, where swift the sea-gull flies
  (Our childhood's home so glad and gay),
Are vanished from our fading eyes,
  And we are strangers far away.

Our kindred rest beneath the shade
  Where breaks and foams the northern wave ;
And thy dear sire, alas ! is laid
  Within a nameless ocean cave.

My heart in silence, year by year,
  Sighs for the past for ever gone ;
And still with thee the flowing tear
  Descends, as darkly time rolls on.

So all our fairest hopes below
  Are wither'd like a hapless flower,
Scatter'd, and torn, and trampled low
  Before the angry autumn shower.

Oh ! then, while fast the moments fly,
  As on the lightning's tireless wing,
May we to Wisdom's voice reply,
  And to the gracious Saviour cling !

Now, while we see around us fall
    The young, the lovely, and the brave,
Oh! may we trust and cherish all
    The hope that rises o'er the grave.

EDINBURGH.

———*o*———

AN ACROSTIC TO I. B.*

I N dewy mornings long ago,
    When summer daisies deck'd the plain,
S weet was thy gladsome voice to me,
    Like music's soothing, sprightly strain.

A rosy smile was on thy cheek,
    A radiant smile of girlish glee,
B eauteous as the star of morn,
    That twinkles o'er the glistening sea.

E very blessing on thy head,
    My darling, gentle Isabel!
L ong, long may peace and happiness
    Within thy bosom richly dwell!

L ike fragrance floating on the wind,
    So may thy moments rise and flow!
A nd may the guiding angels cheer
    And guard and lead thy life below!

* The subject of the above, Isabella Bain, the writer of several elegant little poems, a true friend of the author's, died of small-pox, in the Royal Infirmary, Edinburgh, February 3, 1872, aged 19 years.

B righter and fairer o'er thy path
  May joy and comfort kindly shine,
A lthough thy fate may never be
  To link and blend thy lot with mine.

I n all my passing pilgrimage,
  Where'er my feet may weary wend,
N e'er shall I cease to breathe a prayer,
  That good may still thy steps attend.

MEADOWS, EDINBURGH, 1870.

———o———

A PRECIOUS FLOWER.

AN ACROSTIC.

A PRECIOUS flower I know,
  A maiden meek and fair,
G lad as the roses bright, that glow
  In summer's gentle air.

N o gaudy, weak display
  Has she—no pomp, no pride ;
E very fashion, vain and gay,
  She scorns and lays aside.

S weet as the violet new
  On the green lap of spring,

A ffectionate and pure and true
  To every living thing !

I love her smile sincere,
  Her youth and modesty,
T he lustre of her brown eyes dear,
  So warm with sympathy.

C lothed like the lily fine
  In innocence and grace,
H ow beautiful her features shine
  With virtuous joy and peace !

I f such a precious flower
  Should bloom beneath my care,
S urely with pleasure, hour by hour,
  My kindness she would share.

O h ! may she still enjoy
  The mild, refreshing shower !
N e'er may the blasting storm destroy
  Or stain the precious flower !

EDINBURGH.

SPRING AT ST. BERNARD'S MINERAL WELL, EDINBURGH.

FROM rock to rock, from stone to stone,
 The whirling water dashes on,
And foams along the grassy dell,
And murmurs by St. Bernard's Well!

When wintry floods in fury roar,
And madly, darkly, downward pour,
I love to see them rush and swell
And gurgle near St. Bernard's Well.

And while the Spring returns to shine,
With buds and leaves and blossoms fine,
And verdure crowns the mossy fell,
I hasten to St. Bernard's Well;

While tender, shelter'd April flowers
Adorn the shady slopes and bowers,
And charm me with their fragrant smell
To linger at St. Bernard's Well.

The thorn and willow, green and fair,
Are op'ning to the genial air;
And rhododendrons, rich and gay,
Their tassels to the light display.

And thrilling songs of early love
The blackbirds warble from above,
Enchanting those who toil or dwell
Or wander near St. Bernard's Well.

And soon the Summer's gladd'ning beam
Will fall on terrace, cliff, and stream,
And July's dew and gentle rain
Refresh the herbs and shrubs again.

And thyme, and balm, and London pride,
And pinks, and roses, side by side,
And bright the fuchsia's gaudy bell,
Shall flourish at St. Bernard's Well !

I love to muse with rapture high
Where goats among the daisies lie,
Till evening's soothing sounding bell
Recalls me from St. Bernard's Well.

For there the ancient stately sire,
Warm as a bard with Scottish fire,
Or hermit in his hoary cell,
Delights me at St. Bernard's Well.

EDINBURGH.

———*o*———

SUMMER.

DELIGHTFUL Summer comes again ;
  Her smile is on the bright'ning hills,
  And on the rapid, flashing rills,
And on the distant heaving main.

She comes with blossom for the bee !
  She comes with gladness for the child
  That climbs the craggy mountain wild !
She comes with joy and light for me !

Though I, a stranger, weary, worn,
  Am doom'd to tune my pilgrim lay
  From home and kindred far away,
Like mateless linnet on the thorn ;

Far from Belmungie's shelly shore,
  Far from the cliffs of Cromarty,
  Encircled by the surging sea,
Where tides and billows boil and roar ;

Shine on, sweet Summer, in thy prime !
  I love thy gentle skies and showers,
  I love thy glist'ning leaves and flowers,
In June and July's blooming time.

Though I can stroll and muse no more
   Among the braes at break of day
   (Where Wyvis stands in grandeur grey),
Ardent with rapture, as of yore;

Shine on, sweet Summer! Spread abroad,
   Through Highland glen and Lowland grove,
   Thy kindly smiles of mirth and love,
The tokens of a bounteous God!

That I, with calm and thankful mind,
   May bear with trials, griefs, and woes,
   Until my time of sorrows close,
To His paternal care resigned!

EDINBURGH.

———0———

SHE WORE A PANSY ON HER BREAST.

SHE wore a pansy on her breast—
   A pansy wonderful and rare;
   For it was white, and pure, and fair,
And downy as the pigeon's crest.

She wore a pansy on her breast,
   Her heaving bosom like the sea,
   That swells and sighs so tenderly
When balmy winds are laid to rest.

The pansy, with its comely leaves,
　　And sweet, expressive, purple eye,
　　Blent with a shade of fainter dye,
The sadness of my heart relieves;

And bids me think of gardens bright,
　　And lovely pansies, meek and fine,
　　That in the borders bloom and shine,
And smile beneath the noontide light.

May she who wore the pansy flower
　　A pang of anguish never know;
　　But may she know true joy below,
And comfort in her dying hour!

She met me in the month of May,
　　That matchless maid of modest mien,
　　When skies were clear and trees were green,
And daisies lined the meadow way.

And, like the ' Maid of Athens,' prized
　　And loved by ancient warriors bold,
　　And by the Grecian shores of old
In Byron's song immortalized;

Like starlight on the trembling lake,
　　Her gentle eyes, of mildest blue,
　　A spell upon my spirit threw,
Which did my slumbering lyre awake.

MEADOWS, EDINBURGH, *June* 1872.

BONNY TEENIE BROON.

BONNY Teenie Broon, as she trips alang the street,
   Wi' jinglin' pitchers glancin' clean, an' milk sae
     fresh an' sweet,
Wi' feet as licht an' nimble as the lively mountain roe,
That gaily skips an' dances through the forest an' the snow.

She rises wi' the robin, an' merrily she sings,
While the dew is on the gowan an' the laverock upward
     springs;
An' the licht that plays an' lingers like sunshine on her broo,
Wi' cheery smiles the dowie heart o' sorrow can renew.

Bonny Teenie Broon, frae the country pure an' free,
Whaur loupin' lammies frisk an' run, an' hums the wan-
     derin' bee,
Whaur wuds an' braes are green an' braw, an' fields are
     gay an' fair,
Whaur sparklin' burnies dash and row, an' clover scents
     the air.

Bonny Teenie Broon, in the stoury city's thrang,
Her blithesome heart is saft an' leal the waefu' croods
     amang,
As in the days o' yore, whan she, a bairnie young an' sma',
Gaed gatherin' chuckie-stanes aside the roarin' waterfa'.

H

Bonny Teenie Broon, as the years will slide awa',
Thy shinin' gowden locks may wear the whiteness o' the
    snaw ;
The colour o' the crimson rose may frae thy cheek depart,
An' cloods o' wae an' weariness may settle o'er thy heart.

Bonny Teenie Broon, while youth is on thy side,
An' while the years an' moments like summer streamlets
    glide,
Oh ! prize the priceless Word o' Life, sae precious an'
    divine,
An' seek for truth an' wisdom there, like treasures frae the
    mine.

Its licht will guide thy footsteps through a' the snares o'
    time,
An' lead thee on an' upward to eternal joys sublime ;
Whaur thou shalt rise an' flourish wi' a pure immortal
    bloom,
An' reign an' sing in triumph o'er the darkness o' the tomb.

EDINBURGH.

———*0*———

LITTLE ANNIE'S DEATH.

AN ACROSTIC.

A tender lily, in her earliest bloom,
N ow withered lies in all her fresh perfume,
N o mortal skill her beauty can recall.
I n life's young April, while her soft leaves fall,
E 'en now she slumbers, shrouded in death's gloomy pall.

A las ! the flowers that wither on the plain,
L ilies and violets, will bloom again
I n summer's light, but Annie shall no more
S mile with her sisters on St. Margaret's shore.
O n angel pinions she has passed away,
N ow pure she gladly shines in heaven's clearest ray.

E 'en while a mother shed in melting rain,
L ike Rachel, tears of anguish (all in vain),
D eath came and bore her stainless babe away,
E 'en as the dewdrop, with the light of May,
R ises, expands, and soars to the bright blaze of day.

H er spirit joins the melody sublime,
A nd shares with saints, beyond the breath of time,
Y outh and celestial breath in the immortal clime.

EDINBURGH.

MY CHILDHOOD.

WHILE spring is returning with blossom and flower,
    While sweet birds are singing in forest and
        bower,
While April is streaming o'er mountain and lea,
Oh, Jamie! I think of my childhood and thee.

While night on the city in darkness descends,
I think of departed and long-absent friends;
I think of their faces, so pleasant to me—
Dear Jamie! I think of my childhood and thee.

I think of 'the whins' and the quarry so dear,
And the burn in the den running gentle and clear,
Where the wild pigeon coos on the green hazel tree—
Oh, Jamie! I think of my childhood and thee.

I think of Rosemarkie, its rocks and its braes,
Where we gathered and played in our frolicsome days,
Where we shouted and ran on the shore in our glee—
Oh, Jamie! I think of my childhood and thee.

Oh! sweet was our home, where we ranged without care
While warm summer zephyrs enchanted the air
With the scent of the clover, the broom, and the pea—
Oh, Jamie! I think of my childhood and thee.

But only in dreams now, alas ! I behold
The pine-covered hills where we herded of old,
Where the heather unfolds its red bells to the bee—
Oh, Jamie ! I think of my childhood and thee.

Oh ! far have I roamed from the place of my birth,
But dear to my heart are the woods of the North,
Where the strong Highland breezes blow healthy and free—
Oh, Jamie ! I think of my childhood and thee.

Though my forefathers' dwellings lie lonely and low,
And the friends of my bosom are scatter'd like snow,
Though steep Tomnahurich[1] I never may see,
Dear Jamie ! I think of my childhood and thee.

MEADOWS, EDINBURGH, *April* 1872.

———o———

IN MEMORIAM.

A TRIBUTE TO THE MEMORY OF THE REV. WILLIAM WRIGHTSON, D.D.,

Who died suddenly of fever at Constantinople, November 1, 1872,
after having almost completed a tour of investigation, in view of
organizing an Industrial Christian Mission among the Circassian
refugees in Turkey.

BENEATH a smiling Eastern sky,
Where figs and olives richly shine,
Where roses bloom like things divine,
He meekly laid him down to die.

[1] Where the author's only sister is buried.

By the dark Bosphorus' purple wave,
    Where southern breezes sweetly blow,
    Where green the vine and cypress grow,
The stranger tends his honour'd grave.

Kind hearts will sorrow long and sore,
    For he, the husband and the sire,
    Their help, their comfort, and desire,
Shall greet them by the hearth no more.

And all who love Immanuel's laws,
    Who strive to spread His name abroad,
    May mourn for him, a man of God,
A herald of the glorious cause.

Only a few short months ago
    To home and friends he bade adieu,
    And cross'd the billows broad and blue,
Though age was on his crown and brow.

For strong in faith in God on high,
    And full of love to men below,
    With words of life he longed to go
To tribes who deep in darkness lie.

Weep, weep, 'Adigæ!'[1] ye who roam
    In exile o'er the Turkish plains!

---

[1] 'Adigæ,' the native name of the Circassians, meaning nobles.

He strove to break your grinding chains,
And lead you to a deathless home.

Ye who remember Schamyl's name,
    Your sinking souls he sought to raise,
    To tune Jehovah's holy praise,
And burn with more than patriot flame.

But now he sings the ceaseless psalm,
    Earth's griefs forgot, and toil, and pain ;
    Ours is the loss, but his the gain,
The crown, the glory, and the palm !

EDINBURGH.

————0————

THE STRANGER GRAVE.

WRITTEN AT THE GRAVE OF JOHN GRIGOR, A NATIVE OF
THE BLACK ISLE OF ROSS, WHO DIED IN EDINBURGH,
OCTOBER 2, 1872, AGED SEVENTY-THREE YEARS.

THE wintry clouds are spreading dull and grey
    Along the mountains fading far away,
As thus we sorrow, bending o'er thy breast,
And lay thee in a stranger grave to rest.

Beneath the cedar, gently drooping green,
Where lingering roses beautify the scene,
Thy lonely dust, beneath a stranger sky,
Until the resurrection morn shall lie,

Far from thy dear, thy native northern clime,
Where surging billows lave the rocks sublime ;
Where kindred loved ones rest in death's repose,
And sigh no more beneath a weight of woes.

Frail were thy limbs, thy locks were thin and gray,
Thy youth and manhood long had fled away,
Ere thou didst leave the valleys, fair and green,
Where pass'd with thee life's weary, chequered scene.

Oft hast thou turn'd, with sadly longing soul,
To where the silvery shining waters roll ;
To where the sailor sings with manly glee,
And fisher maidens gaze across the sea.

But thou, O Grigor, shalt behold no more
The hills of Ross, or tread its tranquil shore,
Or gain, alas! what thou would'st fondly crave,
On Avoch's calm sweet braes at last a grave.

Sleep on, sleep on, my countryman, my friend!
The weeping trees their wither'd leaves will blend,
The gentle flowers their summer fragrance shed,
And night winds murmur o'er thy lowly bed.

Sleep on ! Thy slumbering ashes still are dear
To Him who shed by Lazarus' tomb a tear ;
Who gave thee grace His mercy to believe,
Who still the trembling sinner doth receive.

GRANGE CEMETERY, EDINBURGH.

LINES FOR THE FIRST PAGE OF AN ALBUM.

SOPHIA, may thy life be spared
    For many years to come,
And may thy days be richly crown'd
    With all the joys of home !

Thy soul is soft and musical,
    Like streams that flow along
Through summer woods and valleys, full
    Of melody and song.

At thy request the artless bard
    With gladness will bestow
The rude effusions of his heart,
    Upon thy page to glow.

Thy sky may not be always fair ;
    Some drops, alas ! may fall,
And clouds and tempests cross thy path,
    That come indeed to all.

But kindly words and memories
    Will light thy darkest day,
Will freshen up thy fading eye,
    And chase thy griefs away;

Will point thy spirit onward far
  Beyond the dreary night,
While one by one the glimmering stars
  Are fading from thy sight.

EDINBURGH, 1873.

———o———

THE CHILDREN LOVE THE FLOWERS.

THE hero loves his sword of war,
  The maid her rubies bright,
The bard the brilliant blazing star
  That rolls afar in light;
The shepherd loves the lonely grove,
  The sage the silent hours;
But oh! the joyous children love
  The pretty smiling flowers!

Where bold Britannia's mountains stand
  In wild sublimity,
Where brave Columbia's rivers grand
  Roll to the Western sea,
Where Alpine cataracts of foam
  Descend in snowy showers,
And by the Arab's desert home,
  The children love the flowers.

Our little Mary Merrilees,
　So healthy, young, and keen,
Who laughs and dances through the trees
　That grace the meadows green,
Delightful as a fairy queen
　Amid the sylvan bowers,
She roves beneath the summer sheen,
　And oh! she loves the flowers.

The happy, artless children dear,
　God bless and guard them all!
May heaven's holy radiance clear
　Around their footsteps fall!
Oh, may they gain the sheltering shade
　Ere yet the tempest lowers,
And drink of joys that never fade,
　And cull immortal flowers!

When death shall bear my soul away
　Through worlds of light on high,
And in my Father's castle grey
　My harp shall tuneless lie,
Oh! lay me where the woodbines cling,
　By yonder crumbling towers,
Where rosy children run and sing
　And gather purple flowers.

———0———

IN MEMORIAM.

REV. THOMAS GUTHRIE, D.D.

DIED 24TH FEBRUARY 1873, AGED SEVENTY-ONE YEARS.

WE have borne him away, we have laid him to rest,
And the green sod of Scotland is laid on his breast,
On the sunny brae-side, where the primroses spring,
Where the birds of the woodlands in harmony sing.

And the breezes of Scotland will sigh o'er his dust
Until he awake to arise with the just;
And the tears of his country will gather and fall,
Where the green ivy clings to the moss-covered wall.

In hovel and shieling, in palace and hall,
We mourn for our Guthrie, the dearest of all;
Who stood for our Zion undaunted and bold,
Who wept for our woes like the prophets of old.

Our valleys he loved, with their fountains and linns,
Our cities and homes, with their sorrows and sins;
But he will return—ah, never again !
To smile with our rapture or sigh for our pain.

The frail and the fallen, the lost and the poor,
And the orphan he rescued from misery's door,
And the sinner who sailed on destruction's dark wave,
He prayed, and he pleaded, and laboured to save.

But the heart of affection is lifeless and cold,
And the eyes of compassion are dark in the mould;
And the lips of the mighty are silent and chill,
Like the pebbles that lie on the mist-covered hill.

EDINBURGH, *March* 1873.

———o———

LITTLE JOSEPH'S GRAVE.

DOWN in the valley calm and sweet
   Our little Joseph lies;
Oh! silent are his playful feet,
   And dark his azure eyes.

He lies beneath the tender grass,
   Where fall the chilling rains;
Where zephyrs linger as they pass,
   And whisper sad refrains.

Oh! there the oak and holly stand,
   And broom and laurel grow,
And pines and cedars, tall and grand,
   Their sombre shadows throw.

Oh! there the bright laburnum waves
   Its tassels in the air,
And bends in beauty o'er the graves
   When summer days are fair.

And there the rose and myrtle fine
　　Their leaves in autumn shed,
And white convolvuluses twine
　　Their tendrils o'er the dead;

Recalling him who passed away,
　　Our darling infant mild,
To gain the high immortal day,
　　While April blossoms smiled.

EDINBURGH, *November* 1873.

———*o*———

IN MEMORIAM.

REV. DR. CANDLISH.

DIED IN EDINBURGH, OCTOBER 19, 1873.

FAREWELL, bright spirit! thou art gone
　　To mix with kindred souls,
Where high before the Father's throne
　　Angelic music rolls!

Farewell, great spirit! called away
　　From our distracted land,
Where still thy tongue of fire could sway
　　In counsel, and command.

Farewell, our chieftain of renown,
  The faithful and the tried;
While rising wars and dangers frown,
  Oh! who like thee shall guide?

Sweet is thy rest beyond the tide;
  But mourning Zion sighs,
While thou hast laid thine arms aside,
  And won the victor's prize.

EDINBURGH, *October* 25, 1873.

———*o*———

IN MEMORIAM.

JEMIMA TAYLOR.

The author's only sister died at Inverness, November 12, 1871, aged thirty-two years, and lies buried there in Tomnahurich Cemetery.

BENEATH the mossy mountain sod,
  Beneath the heather's gladd'ning glow,
  Where thyme and blue-bells blend and blow,
Thou sleepest low in death's abode.

The breeze that stirs the Highland lake,
  And through the sounding forest plays,
  The pines' and birchen branches sways,
Till o'er thy dust they bend and shake.

While weary on a stranger strand,
  My dearest thoughts are still with thee,
  Though thou to me shalt silent be
Until I reach the spirit-land.

The fond affection of thy soul,
  Thy fadeless faith and kindly care,
  No more shall I profusely share
While waves of woe around me roll.

The autumn leaf was in the wane,
  The flowers in desolation lay,
  When thou didst pine and pass away,
And leave me thus to sigh in pain.

We parted when the corn was green,
  I left my home to toil for years;
  When I returned it was with tears,
For death was now where life had been.

Beneath thy mother's yearning eye
  The roses vanished from thy cheek,
  And thou didst die, serene and meek,
While I, alas ! could not be nigh.

I went—I saw thee changed to clay ;
  Beneath the sod I laid thee down,
  Where none are near thy grave to own,
And breathe thy name from day to day.

But, thanks to Christ, the day will come,
   For which His people long and pray,
   When we shall meet at break of day,
And gather in our Father's home.

Till then, by love and grief combined,
   Like scent of withered violets dear,
   Thy mem'ry I shall keep and wear
Within my inmost heart enshrined.

EDINBURGH, *March* 1874.

———*0*———

IN MEMORIAM.

DAVID LIVINGSTONE,

THE GREAT AFRICAN MISSIONARY, EXPLORER, AND PHILAN-
THROPIST, BURIED IN WESTMINSTER ABBEY, 18TH
APRIL 1874.

BRITANNIA! weep, and meekly bow the head;
   Receive and gather to his noble rest,
   Among the mighty, on thy grateful breast,
From dangers numberless, the faithful dead,

Until the trumpet of the angel bright,
   With piercing echoes through creation round,
   Shall rouse his relics from the dark profound
To life immortal with the Lord in light.

I

Where mildly, solemnly, and dimly falls
    The streaming light on column, aisle, and nave,
    There lay thy Livingstone in glory's grave,
Within the Abbey's consecrated walls.

There let his ashes calm in slumber lie,
    Where sages, bards, and conquering heroes sleep;
    A precious seed, while we the harvest reap,
Although we sorrow when the deathless die.

Britannia! linger not; he bids thee rise,
    And forward to the field of promise go,
    The gospel grain afar and wide to sow,
And free the slave that sad in bondage sighs.

He tracks the fevered swamp and river wild
    With patient heart and weary feet no more,
    The distant silent jungle to explore,
And bring salvation to the savage child.

Far from his native hills of purple heath,
    By Bangweolo's deep and lonely wave,
    Tended and loved by dusky strangers brave,
He died, and gained the pilgrim-martyr's wreath.

While generations rise and ages roll,
    His name (while freedom's glorious heralds run)
    Shall light the Negro's hearth from sire to son,
And glad the good and bold from pole to pole.

EDINBURGH, *May* 1874.

MESSRS. MOODY AND SANKEY'S EDINBURGH FAREWELL MEETING,

HELD NEAR 'HUNTER'S BOG,' QUEEN'S PARK, ON THURSDAY,
21ST MAY 1874.

UPON the cold, steep, rugged mountain slope,
 Beneath a scowling sky,
They told the words of everlasting hope
 To thousands gathered nigh,—

To thousands gathered in the upland glen
 Beneath the rocky brow,
To sires and mothers, bairns and stalwart men,
 And maids with hearts aglow.

While briny breezes from the Northern Sea
 Blew dreary, keen, and chill,
The people stream'd along the lonely lea,
 And o'er the craggy hill,

To hear once more the words of love and power,
 And sing the solemn strains,
Which long shall cheer us, like the tranquil showers
 Of July's balmy rains.

Oh! it was grand and glorious to behold
 The vast assembly there,
Met, like our fathers in the wilds of old,
 Beneath the evening air.

And glad were they, brave champions of our God,
   Come from the distant West,
To stand on Scotland's covenanted sod,
   Where many martyrs rest,

The gospel boldly, freely to declare,
   Which long has clearly rung;
Amidst our Caledonian valleys fair,
   Through men of thunder tongue.

Oh, there were prayers and praises which awoke
   The echoes of the dell ;
Oh, there were sobs and raptures while they spoke,
   And tears at their farewell.

They leave Edina's classic homes and halls,
   And Scotia's ancient shore,
Soon to return to toil where duty calls,
   Beyond the billows' roar.

But joyful thousands through our city throngs
   Have learned to trust the Lord,
Have learned to pray, and sing sweet Sion's songs,
   And love Jehovah's word.

Oh, let us join our Jesus to extol,
   Our Saviour, strength, and shield !
He hath revived His people as of old ;
   His glory is revealed.

Oh, may His kingdom flourish and extend
  Among the nations wide,
Until His foes before His mercy bend,
  And rally on His side !

Oh, may His Church our native isles within
  Through ages still endure,
And win and save the hosts of hell and sin
  By life and lustre pure ;

Till He shall come, her glory and delight,
  Her Shepherd, King, and Friend,
With clouds and thunders, and His armies bright,
  Her wars and woes to end !

EDINBURGH, *June* 1874.

————0————

PATRIOTIC LINES WRITTEN IN AUTUMN.

AN ACROSTIC.

M Y soul is full of pleasant rhymes,
    While autumn winds are on the wold,
    While skies are growing grey and cold,
  And bells are ringing evening chimes.

A lthough the past, like morning's sheen
    Of purple, gold, and sapphire hue,
    Has early fled, I love to view
The tender flowers and valleys green.

R ing, ring, ye bells, at evening's close,
    While shadows o'er the Garden fall,
    While sunset gilds the Castle wall,
And drowsy songsters find repose.

Y our mellow tones my life inspire ;
    Your swelling streams of music calm
    Come o'er me like a holy psalm,
And warm me with immortal fire.

C ome evening, with thy dusky shades
    And mingling gleams of parting light,
    When Luna, lustrous queen of night,
Shines mildly o'er the dewy glades.

O h ! hours of rapture pure and sweet,
    When labour rests its weary oar,
    When musing bards transported soar,
And waiting saints their Saviour meet.

M y country ! while thy hills I see,
    Where wildly blooms the azure bell,
    And should I bid thy shores farewell,
My heart shall fondly throb for thee.

M y rustic harp is rudely worn,
    Its strings are trembling with decay ;
    But still thy fame my muse shall sway,
Though I should warble strains forlorn.

O land of ancient deathless song !
    O land of martyrs, bright and true !
    May none the loyal hearts subdue
Which round thy stately standard throng !

N e'er may the star of freedom fair
    Along thy borders cease to smile ;
    And may thy peace, majestic isle,
Be shielded by celestial care !

EAST PRINCES STREET GARDENS,
EDINBURGH, *August* 1874.

———*0*———

SACRED PIECES.

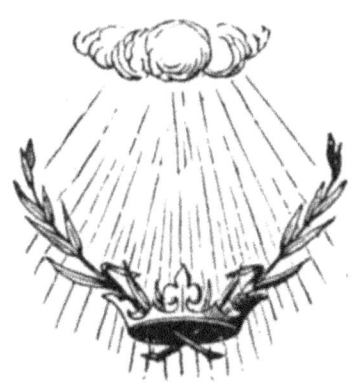

NEW YEAR'S HYMN, 1860.

'Awake, sweet harp of Judah, 'wake,
Retune thy strings for Jesus' sake.'
HENRY KIRKE WHITE.

O FATHER, Son, and Holy Ghost,
Our God, we come to Thee,
To bless Thy name for sparing us
Another year to see;

For guiding us and shielding us,
Frail creatures of the clay,
Through many dark and rugged scenes,
And many a weary way;

While many in the year that's gone
  Are called from time away,—
Their spirits to Thy judgment throne,
  Their bodies to the clay.

None other know what is to come,
  But Thou, Almighty One;
And ere another year will pass,
  Our glasses may be run.

Eternal Spirit, fill our hearts
  With life and love divine,
That we may love Thee in return,
  And keep those laws of Thine.

Incline our wandering youthful hearts
  To seek Thy precious face,
While we are still on mercy's ground,
  And at a throne of grace.

Oh, may Thy grace support our souls
  While we are wandering here,
And may Thy glorious countenance
  Dispel each rising fear.

Then upward, onward we will go,
  Our path by Thee made plain;
Thyself our life and light while here,
  And death our endless gain.

RADDERY.

PRAYER FOR AN INFANT.

AN ACROSTIC.

J esus, kind Saviour, condescend to shine,
A nd bless the little one with grace divine;
N ow, in her tender years, oh, may she be
E arly united in her soul to Thee.

U nder Thy wings may she for ever rest,
R eclining meekly on Thy loving breast;
Q uietly and closely walking by Thy side,
U ntil she reach her home beyond death's tide.

H appy are they who sing around Thy throne,
A ll their wild fightings and dark fears are gone:
R eturning storms their spirits cannot bend;
T heir joys shall flow celestial without end.

RADDERY, 28th December 1860.

———o———

'WATCH AND PRAY.'

MATT. XXVI. 41.

WHEN Jesus left this world below,
 And to the Father went away,
His dear disciples He did show
 How they had need to 'watch and pray.'

'Fightings without and fears within'
 Would press their spirits day by day;
If they would conquer hell and sin,
 They ceaselessly must 'watch and pray.'

He knew the dangers of the road,
 The snares which round them darkly lay,
To draw their souls from peace with God,
 If they forgot to 'watch and pray.'

While thus *He* did them teach and train
 To feel themselves poor sinful clay,
They clearly saw, if they would gain
 The crown, they still must 'watch and pray.'

Peter denied his Master thrice—
 With oaths and frowns he answered, 'Nay;'
But ere the cock-crow sounded twice,
 He felt his need to 'watch and pray.'

And still the artful tempter tries
    Frail, helpless ones aside to sway ;
Blest is the man who humbly cries
    For constant grace to ' watch and pray.'

Our minds, how fast and far they rove,
    Like thoughtless children wild at play !
Lord, give us wisdom from above,
    That we may learn to ' watch and pray.'

Almighty Saviour ! grant us grace,
    Our doubts and sins and sorrows slay ;
Till, safe at last before Thy face,
    We need no more to ' watch and pray.'

FALLS OF TRUIM.

———0———

AN ACROSTIC.

TO A. U., CROMARTY.

A LIGHT divine for ever shines
    Along the narrow road
That leads the weary, longing soul
    To glory and to God.

N ow through a world of snares and death
 Poor pilgrims we must go ;
 But when we reach our Father's house,
 With joy our souls shall glow.

D arkness, and care, and grief, and woe,
 We then shall all lay down,
 That we may wear a spotless robe
 And a celestial crown.

R edemption through our Saviour's blood
 We then shall understand,
 When we shall drink the purest joys
 Which flow from His right hand.

E ternally we shall adore
 His mercy, love, and grace,
 Who takes us from distress and sin
 To endless life and peace.

W hile here below we may abide,
 Lord, help us night and day
 To walk in purity and truth,
 And never fall or stray.

RADDERY, *July* 1863.

————o————

IN MEMORIAM.

REV. JAMES KENNEDY, INVERNESS, 1863.

'Precious in the sight of the Lord is the death of
His saints.'—DAVID.

THE Master calls the servant home
    To the eternal rest;
His body slumbers with the just,
    His soul soars with the blest.

He tired not of the glorious work,
    His Saviour's work of love;
He only leaves the cross below
    To wear the crown above.

His aged face and hoary hairs
    Shone with the smile of heaven,
For faith and hope and love divine
    To him were richly given.

On earth he gladly would remain,
    To toil, and preach, and pray;
But sweeter was the welcome call—
    'Good servant, come away!'

'FEED MY SHEEP.'

JOHN XXI. 16; ACTS XX. 28.

INSCRIBED TO REV. GEORGE TAYLOR, M.A.

IT is the Master's parting words
　　To His beloved band—
A holy mandate left below,
　　A sweet, divine command,

That they who o'er the Master's fold
　　Affection's vigils keep,
Are bound to feed the ' Church of God,'
　　The glorious Master's sheep.

Among the mountains dark and wild,
　　Where lost ones blindly stray,
The watchman still must sound the horn
　　Along the homeward way,

That wayward wanderers may return
　　From dangers manifold,
And walk with those who safely feed
　　And rest within the fold.

A noble charge—the most sublime
　　To sinful mortal given,
To be a servant of *the Lord*,
　　A messenger of Heaven!

Be thine to watch and pray and feed
　While useless hirelings sleep,
And guard from fierce, infernal wolves
　'The little flock,' 'the sheep.'

Fame is a passing ray, that melts
　Like morning's light away,
And earthly crowns shall moulder down
　And perish in the clay ;

But lasting as eternity
　(Though now they sigh and weep)
Shall be the boundless, holy joy
　Of those who feed the sheep.

WEST CALDER.

———o———

SPIRITUAL DARKNESS AND PERPLEXITY.

Ps. CII. 6, CXLIII. 2, CXXX. 6.

BENEATH the dreary sky,
　Amid the desert wild,
Bewildered, Lord, am I,
　Thy weary, wandering child.

The wolves are now abroad,
  The storm is dark and high;
Help me, my Saviour God,
  Before I sink and die.

Why did I blindly roam
  Afar from joy and rest?
Why did I leave my home,
  Sweet Jesus, near Thy breast?

Alas! no kindly ray
  To guide my steps appears;
From safety far away,
  I groan with doubts and fears.

I sigh amidst the gloom
  Of deep and starless night,
Sad as the doleful tomb,
  For Thee, my sun and light.

The anguish of my soul
  To Thee is only known,
While dreadful thunders roll
  Around me here alone.

Could I the peace recall
  Which from my breast is flown,
Which did my life enthral
  While I Thy love did own,

My sorrow would subside,
　My path be plain and bright,
And danger by my side
　Could never more affright.

Alas ! my faithless heart,
　So feeble and forlorn,
Is by the tempter's art
　Through fierce confusion borne.

And human might is vain
　To succour, shield, or save
From sin's perplexing pain,
　And ruin's rising wave.

While thus I pine and sigh
　In hopeless misery,
My languid, weeping eye
　Is dimly turned to Thee.

My Lord ! Thy grace display,
　My spirit to restore ;
Oh ! bear my guilt away ;
　Oh ! bid me stray no more.

MEADOWS, EDINBURGH, 1874.

HYMN—'PREPARE TO MEET THY GOD.'

Written while meditating on the fearful railway collision which occurred at Manuel Junction, near Linlithgow, on Tuesday morning, 26th January 1874, causing the sudden death of 17 persons, including Lydia Wilson, Cromarty, and Margaret Lindsay, Aberdeen, young Christian friends of the Author.

THE sound of dread eternity
    In thunder tones appeals to thee.
O brother, brother, ready be—
    Prepare, 'Prepare to meet thy God!'

The dead in Jesus gone before
Await us on the holy shore;
Awake, arise, and sleep no more—
    Prepare, 'Prepare to meet thy God!'

The voice of Jesus lovingly
In mercy calleth, 'Come to me!'
Oh! sinner, sinner, hear and flee—
    Prepare, 'Prepare to meet thy God!'

Behold, backslider, still for thee
His precious blood and grace are free;
Oh! from thy chains releasèd be—
    Prepare, 'Prepare to meet thy God!'

EDINBURGH, *February* 1874.

HYMN.

HOLY Father, God on high,
    Hear and bless me when I cry !
While my soul to thee I raise,
Oh receive my simple praise !

Great, immortal, matchless King !
Saints and angels gaze and sing,
And Thy glory bright adore,
As they stand Thy face before.

Let me join the deathless strain,
Loud and boundless as the main ;
Let me of their joy partake,
For my precious Saviour's sake.

While the silent circles run,
Years and moments one by one,
Let me at Thy footstool fall,
Let me hear Thy gracious call.

Holy Spirit, Light divine,
On my darkness rise and shine ;
Sanctify my sinful heart,
And Thy grace to me impart.

Lead me, while I linger here,
Loving Shepherd, in Thy fear ;
Bring me, when my seasons close,
In Thy presence to repose.

EDINBURGH.

THE END.

MURRAY AND GIBB, EDINBURGH,
PRINTERS TO HER MAJESTY'S STATIONERY OFFICE.

www.ingramcontent.com/pod-product-compliance
Lightning Source LLC
Chambersburg PA
CBHW080830250626
47160CB00008B/2893